THE
PURSUIT
OF CHRISTIAN
MATURITY

THE
PURSUIT
OF CHRISTIAN
MATURITY

FLOURISHING
IN THE GRACE
AND KNOWLEDGE
OF CHRIST

A.W.
TOZER

COMPILED AND EDITED BY JAMES L. SNYDER

BETHANYHOUSE
a division of Baker Publishing Group
Minneapolis, Minnesota

© 2024 by International Literary Properties, LLC

Published by Bethany House Publishers
Minneapolis, Minnesota
BethanyHouse.com

Bethany House Publishers is a division of
Baker Publishing Group, Grand Rapids, Michigan

Library of Congress Cataloging-in-Publication Data
Names: Tozer, A. W. (Aiden Wilson), 1897–1963, author. | Snyder, James L., author. Title: The pursuit of Christian maturity : flourishing in the grace and knowledge of
Christ / A. W. Tozer and James L. Snyder.
Description: Minneapolis, Minnesota : Bethany House Publishers, a division of
Baker Publishing Group, [2024]
Identifiers: LCCN 2023054032 | ISBN 9780764240300 (paper) | ISBN 9780764243240 (cloth) | ISBN 9781493446650 (ebook)
Subjects: LCSH: Christian life. | Spiritual life—Christianity.
Classification: LCC BV4501.3 .T6995 2024 | DDC 248.4—dc23/eng/20240221
LC record available at https://lccn.loc.gov/2023054032

Scripture quotations are from the King James Version of the Bible.

Cover design by Rob Williams
Cover image from Shutterstock

James L. Snyder is represented by The Steve Laube Agency.

24 25 26 27 28 29 30   7 6 5 4 3 2 1

CONTENTS

Introduction   7

1. The First Steps toward Christian Maturity   11
2. The Challenge of Christian Maturity   23
3. The Opposition of Christian Maturity   33
4. The Enemy of Christian Maturity   43
5. The Growth of Christian Maturity   51
6. The Inward Passion for Christian Maturity   61
7. The Price of Christian Maturity   69
8. The Components of Christian Maturity   77
9. The Completeness of Christian Maturity   85
10. The Will of God in Christian Maturity   93
11. The Heart of Christian Maturity   103
12. The Focus of Christian Maturity   113
13. The Threats to Christian Maturity   121
14. The Clouds Hindering Christian Maturity   131
15. The Self-Trust Danger to Christian Maturity   139

16. Temptations Boost Christian Maturity 147
17. The Environment of Christian Maturity 155
18. An Important Door to Christian Maturity 163
19. The Devil's Attack on Christian Maturity 169
20. Living in the Fullness of Christian Maturity 177
21. The Triumph of Christian Maturity 183

Further Reading 189

INTRODUCTION

From the beginning of A.W. Tozer's conversion, he was passionate about his relationship with God. He didn't allow anything or anyone to come between him and his Creator. That is the focus of this book, based on sermons on this subject.

Throughout *The Pursuit of Christian Maturity*, Dr. Tozer quotes from one of his favorite books, *The Cloud of Unknowing*. Second only to the Bible, this book was his constant companion. The author is anonymous, unknown to us, and wrote the book over six hundred years ago, yet Tozer felt the book held within its pages an important message for modern-day Christians.

At the outset, Tozer refers to something in the book that seems strange for an author to say. The author of *The Cloud of Unknowing* didn't want just anyone to read his book. He states, "Now among those that I don't want to read the book clearly are the fleshly jangles. That is idle talkers, people who chatter all the time. Open praisers and blamers of themselves and others. Open praisers and blamers of themselves, don't bother, if you're not fit you'll never come anywhere. And the tellers of trifle don't bother coming around this group."

He believed that many who considered themselves Christian would not be able to understand the message he was giving, and it would be useless for them even to try reading it. But even if they started to read it, they would soon lose interest in the subject and give up.

Tozer points out that in *The Cloud of Unknowing*, the author divides Christians into several categories. Of the different types, I will focus on the carnal Christian and the mature Christian. These two define the essence of spiritual maturity I'd like to emphasize. Understanding these two categories will go a long way toward addressing the issue of Christian maturity, or lack thereof, in our day.

The world, the flesh, and the devil motivate the carnal Christian. The devil tricks them into believing they're all right spiritually. Tozer said that if the evangelical, fundamentalist Church didn't get its act together within fifty years, it would become liberal. It has been over sixty years since he died, and boy was he right. The Christian Church today is more reflective of the culture than it has ever been since the days of the apostles. This was the great concern of Tozer, and I believe it should be our concern as well today.

"Esaias also crieth concerning Israel, Though the number of the children of Israel be as the sand of the sea, a remnant shall be saved" (Romans 9:27). Much like *The Cloud of Unknowing*, this book by Tozer centers on mature Christians, whom he thought would be the only ones able to fully understand and appreciate its teaching. Those in the carnal Christian category would most likely not be interested.

Another quote that fascinated Tozer, taken from the same ancient book, was "He is a jealous lover and suffereth no rival." This truth was very important to Tozer, and so he talked a lot about the need to clear away anything and everything that stands between God and us, no matter what it is. This is often the hardest part to deal with in our growing relationship with God, and only a mature Christian can do so. The carnal Christian wouldn't see the need nor the urgency in having to clear away any obstacles, probably because they don't view them as such.

But it seems Tozer's favorite quote from *The Cloud of Unknowing* is "Look now forward and let be backward." He was fascinated with this motto, and in this book, you will hear him explain the concept well. He believed these words to be the key to a healthy, mature Christian experience. I appreciate how Tozer uses the phrase in this regard. I won't say it is Tozer at his best, but it sure comes close.

Tozer's ability to take a book that was written more than six centuries ago and make it understandable and relevant today is remarkable. Personally, the motto "Look now forward and let be backward" has significantly impacted my Christian experience.

Again, Tozer says that the carnal Christian would not be able to understand the meaning of what he was teaching here. Much of life as a Christian is based on the past. Tozer's advice is "let be backward." In other words, let the past be the past, and press forward in the power and grace of the Holy Spirit. If I dwell on my past, I am robbing God. Tozer makes that very clear in this book. And by the time the reader reaches the final page, they'll begin to understand just how much this can affect our Christian maturity.

I especially like what Tozer says in chapter 15: "If you reflect on your life in prayer and write down on a pad of paper what you believe are your virtues, in truth those are your weaknesses. Those very virtues are your sources of trouble. The only way to deal with this is to look to God and stop thinking about yourself." The carnal Christian is more concerned with what pleases them, whereas the mature Christian focuses only on what pleases God. That is the major difference between the two.

Finally, throughout this book, Tozer emphasizes the truth that entertainment robs God of what is rightfully His. This is another failure among carnal Christians. Paul's bold testimony, then, should also be ours—those of us who are striving toward Christian maturity: "I die daily" (1 Corinthians 15:31).

Dr. James L. Snyder

THE FIRST STEPS TOWARD
CHRISTIAN MATURITY

As the hart panteth after the water brooks, so panteth my soul after thee, O God. My soul thirsteth for God, for the living God: when shall I come and appear before God?

Psalm 42:1–2

Everything begins somewhere and at some time. In thinking about Christian maturity, we need to start at the very beginning. As John begins his gospel, he says, "In the beginning was the Word, and the Word was with God, and the Word was God" (John 1:1).

Beginnings are crucial because they lay the foundation for the journey toward the final goal. Christian maturity is the ultimate goal, which starts in this life but does not end here. It continues into the next—into eternity. It's a process I'm unsure how to comprehend, but it's continuous. What matters most as I mature in Christ is where I am in that process.

I was not always a Christian. When my family moved to Akron, Ohio, it was a changing point in my life. My family was not Christian; we did not go to church and, of course, did not read the Bible. We were just hardworking people trying to make a living during the First World War.

As a teenager, I worked at a rubber factory in Akron. One day when I was walking home, a crowd gathered across the street to hear somebody who was preaching. I thought, *Doesn't that man have a church to preach in? What's he doing over there? It isn't even Sunday.*

Not understanding what was happening, my curiosity got the best of me, and I crossed the street for a closer examination. The man was German, his accent hard to understand, so I decided I needed to get closer.

I was startled by what he said: "If you don't know how to be saved, just call on God, saying, 'God, be merciful to me, a sinner,' and God will hear you." That awakened within me a hunger for God I never had before. I did not understand it and therefore couldn't anticipate what was about to happen to me.

When I got home, I went straight up to the attic where I could be alone and think all this out. Many things happened that afternoon as I wrestled with God, but ultimately, I stepped into the attic a lost sinner but came out a believing Christian. Of course, I didn't completely understand what it all meant at the time.

One of the first things I did was buy a Bible. Our family had no Bible, so I was the first to own one. I brought it home and spent time reading it. I must confess there was a lot I was reading I did not quite understand. Much of it didn't make sense to me, but something within me cultivated a passion for God that could only be satiated by seeking Him in the Word.

My passion for God changed my life from that point onward. Each day I discovered something about God I could not understand or explain. I was beginning to appreciate what David meant when he said, "As the hart panteth after the water brooks, so panteth my soul after thee." I was developing a strong desire for knowing God that could not be satisfied with anything else.

Over the years, I realized that my zeal for God was the primary thing ruling my life. Not a burning desire to work for God, but a passionate desire to know and please God. Everything else fell by the wayside, and my concentration focused on getting to know God personally and deeply. This is all there is to it.

Not only did I start reading my Bible, but I also started attending church, which inspired me to follow Christ. I could not get enough Bible reading or churchgoing. I also encouraged my parents to attend church and often talked to them about my passion for Christ, and eventually they both came to know Christ as their Lord and Savior.

I did not know much about being a Christian, but I was zealous about finding out more, no matter what it cost me. This became the number one priority in my life.

As I progressed in my Christian experience, I became filled with the Holy Spirit. This gave me a deeper passion and a power I had not experienced before. I have been climbing the ladder of Christian maturity ever since those early days.

Now, after being a Christian for over forty years, I have come to a painful conclusion. Most present-day Christians live a sub-Christian life. These Christians are not joyful because they are not holy, and they are not holy because they are not filled with the Holy Spirit. And they're not filled with the Holy Spirit because they are not separated persons. The Spirit cannot fill those whom He cannot separate, and those whom He cannot make holy, He cannot make happy. True happiness comes from an inner experience with God. That is the dilemma of Christianity today.

According to the Bible, the modern Christian is typically not Christlike. They are not one with Christ, and the proof lies in serious spiritual flaws among today's children of God. Modern Christians are bogged down by their moral weaknesses, frequent defeats, and dulled understanding. To a large degree, they're living outside the will of God, unconcerned with what the Scriptures have to say about what it means to seek God and love Him with all of their hearts.

This substandard condition among many Christians today is not unfamiliar in the Bible. Remember what was said about Israel, God's people in the Old Testament, and repeated in the New Testament? "Yet the number of the children of Israel shall be as the sand of the sea, which cannot be measured nor numbered; and it shall come to pass, that in the place where it was said unto them, Ye are not my people, there it shall be said unto them, Ye are the sons of the living God" (Hosea 1:10).

And in the New Testament, we read: "Of whom we have many things to say, and hard to be uttered, seeing ye are dull of hearing. For when for the time ye ought to be teachers, ye have need that one teach you again which be the first principles of the oracles of God; and are become such as have need of milk, and not of strong meat" (Hebrews 5:11–12).

In the book of Revelation, in the seven letters to the churches, we have conditions laid before us of churches functioning as churches, but they have lost their first love, are cold, and have much wrong with them spiritually. Our Lord said, "And because iniquity shall abound, the love of many shall wax cold" (Matthew 24:12). Later, Jesus stated, "Nevertheless I have somewhat against thee, because thou hast left thy first love" (Revelation 2:4). That should be a great warning to Christians today.

The apostle Paul admonished the Corinthian church about this very issue of spiritual maturity. I wonder, would he similarly admonish Christians in the Church today? "And I, brethren, could not speak unto you as unto spiritual, but as unto carnal, even as unto babes in Christ. I have fed you with milk, and not with meat: for hitherto ye were not able to bear it, neither yet now are ye able. For ye are yet carnal: for whereas there is among you envying, and strife, and divisions, are ye not carnal, and walk as men?" (1 Corinthians 3:1–3).

The book *The Cloud of Unknowing* contains a prayer that has inspired my life: "God, unto whom all hearts be open, and unto whom all will speaketh, and unto whom no privy thing is hid. I beseech Thee so for to cleanse the intent of mine heart with the unspeakable gift of Thy grace, that I may perfectly love Thee, and worthily praise Thee. Amen."

The words "God, unto whom all hearts be open" remind us that the Lord is able to see into the heart of each person, even if they attempt to close it, lock it, and throw away the key. God can see into your heart as if it were standing wide

15

open. One of the doctrines of the Bible, not much heard these days but strongly emphasized in *The Cloud of Unknowing*, is that the will of a person's heart is their prayer. What you will in your heart is eloquent, and God is able to hear what you are willing to do and what you are determined to do— what it is you're planning in your heart. "And unto whom no privy [secret] thing is hid."

Do you see any theological fault with this prayer? If this sounds extreme and fanatical, you ought to be born again, for the true child of God will say amen to this desire to more perfectly love God, ready and willing to worship Him with all that they are.

And prayer is among the most essential and effective workings in the Christian's heart. James Montgomery said it best when he wrote:

> "Prayer is the soul's sincere desire,
> Unuttered or expressed;
> The motion of a hidden fire
> That trembles in the breast."

The author of *The Cloud of Unknowing* warned those people into whose hands this little book came to be held, "Now I charge thee and I beseech thee in the name of the Father and of the Son and of the Holy Spirit, that thou neither read this book, nor write it, nor speak it, nor suffer it to be read, written or spoken of by any except such as has true will and whole intent. Purpose for him is to be a perfect follower of Christ. Not only in active living but in this kind of contemplative living it is possible by grace to become in this present life a perfect soul yet abiding in a mortal body."

Strangely, the author didn't want just anybody reading his book unless they had a genuine and deep desire to know God. This was not a book to read for mere amusement; it presented a passion for Christian maturity. Readers with an entertainment mindset would not understand what the book was saying at its core.

But why would any author ask somebody *not* to read his book? As I studied *The Cloud of Unknowing*, and as I grew spiritually, I began to understand the author's purpose in writing it. The challenge presented in the book was only for Christians who shared the same kind of passion for Christ the author had. Thus the book was not something meant to entertain.

Today, if you want a book to sell millions of copies, it must have an overriding entertainment element. But this book by an unknown author contains no entertainment value whatsoever. In fact, in some areas it is rather challenging.

This is not something new. Jesus understood how it was in His day, and it was obvious that some people couldn't accept the teaching of Jesus. Therefore, He disguised His teaching a little so as to speak to those who were able and willing to hear it. I'm not suggesting, of course, that He was deceiving anyone; rather, He was giving His teaching a kind of spiritual code, so that the ones who could get it, got it, and the ones who did not get it, didn't. It was as if He were keeping it back from certain ones.

We refer to this type of teaching as parable. In Matthew 13:10–16, the disciples came to Jesus and asked Him why He spoke in parables. Jesus explained that His message was for those who could hear His words, understand them, and apply them to their lives. That is the work of the Holy Spirit.

The same thing applied to the apostle Paul when he wrote, "And I, brethren, could not speak unto you as unto spiritual, but as unto carnal, even as unto babes in Christ. I have fed you with milk, and not with meat; for hitherto ye were not able to bear it, neither yet now are ye able" (1 Corinthians 3:1–2). It wasn't that Paul did not want them to hear his message; instead, they could not hear it. In other words, Paul said, "I can't give it to you because you can't take it."

In essence, what the author of *The Cloud of Unknowing* is saying is that "I don't want anybody bothering with this unless you have made up your mind and have a genuine intent, having purposed in your heart to be a true follower of Christ." The author wasn't interested in how many people were reading his book. On the contrary, he wanted the right people with the right heart not only to read his book, but also to apply what it was saying to their everyday lives.

In modern times, many feel we must pull the preaching of the Word down to the level of the ignorant and most spiritually obtuse. We must tell entertaining stories and crack jokes in order to capture their attention and ensure they continue to come back for more. Sadly, that is where we are today.

Why do we pull the gospel down, addressing the carnal and cheapest saints who hang on with their dainty teeth to the kingdom of God instead of those who are genuinely thirsting after God? Unfortunately, very little today is addressed to the mature Christian.

Suppose the author of *The Cloud of Unknowing* was here with me. I can hear him saying, "By the grace of God and the power of the Trinity, I beseech you, don't write about this unless people are determined in their hearts to be perfect followers of Christ." I pray and hope that we may be worthy to read this so that by the intent of our heart we may perfectly love God and praise Him and by His grace follow Him to the greatest point possible in this life.

The Christian life has a definite beginning point, but contrary to what we hear today, that is just the start. Many people talk about how and where they were born again. I rejoice in that and delight in anybody who has come to know Jesus Christ as their Lord and Savior. I enjoy hearing testimonies of salvation. But rarely do I hear testimonies about a life growing and developing in the grace of God. Too many are today what they were when they first became a Christian, and I cannot tell you how sad that makes me feel.

I have never given more time, prayer, and painstaking attention than to the subject of Christian maturity. Because I did, and because it is so important, I felt Satan attempting to thwart the purpose of God in my life and ministry. I think, too, he has thwarted the purpose of God in some other people's lives. At times I sensed I was in raw contact with hell itself.

I do not ask God for some things, and I do not want them. I do ask for other things. The one thing I have asked of Him in recent years is that I might be a seer. There are so many unseeing people in Christianity that I want to be someone who sees. I want to understand and have discernment and know the whole plan of God. I am not referring to prophecy; I'm referring to being able to appraise any situation and see it as God sees it and know what He thinks of it and also know what to do about it—understanding what the will of God is amid all the religious confusion.

Becoming a Christian was the beginning of my journey toward Christian maturity. It will never be completed in this life, and I look forward to how it works in the life to come, in the presence of my Lord.

As David's hart panted after the water brooks, my life has been an ongoing panting after God himself. Nothing else satisfies me, and I will not stop longing for God, as I can never get enough of Him.

What about you? If you have read this far, please stop and seriously think about what you have read. Do you have a genuine passion for God? Are you willing to go forward despite the oppression from the enemy?

We often hear that the battle is the Lord's, but what we don't hear is that He fights those battles through us. The devil cannot touch God, but he surely can touch you. Are you willing to pay the price of Christian maturity?

Dear Lord Jesus, how my heart yearns for Thee in all Thy glory. To know Thee is to love Thee in ways I cannot truly comprehend. I praise Thee and seek Thee with all my heart. Praise Your holy name. Amen.

WHEN I SURVEY
THE WONDROUS CROSS

When I survey the wondrous cross
on which the Prince of glory died,
my richest gain I count but loss,
and pour contempt on all my pride.

Forbid it, Lord, that I should boast
save in the death of Christ, my God!
All the vain things that charm me most,
I sacrifice them through his blood.

See, from his head, his hands, his feet,
sorrow and love flow mingled down.
Did e'er such love and sorrow meet,
or thorns compose so rich a crown?

Were the whole realm of nature mine,
that were a present far too small.
Love so amazing, so divine,
demands my soul, my life, my all.

Isaac Watts

THE CHALLENGE OF CHRISTIAN MATURITY

But grow in grace, and in the knowledge of our Lord and Saviour Jesus Christ. To him be glory both now and for ever. Amen.

2 Peter 3:18

Every Christian certainly faces a significant challenge as they grow in the grace and knowledge of our Lord and Savior Jesus Christ. We know where that challenge comes from; it is Satan himself. He cannot "unsave" anybody, but he can make the maturing experience a terrible and defeating one for many.

Yet our own people present another challenge. The writer of *The Cloud of Unknowing* understood that certain people would drastically challenge the spiritual growth of others among the people of God. These are the people he did not want to read his book. He states, "Now among those that I don't want to read the book clearly are the fleshly jangles. That is idle talkers, people who chatter all the time. Open praisers and blamers of themselves and others. Open praisers and blamers of themselves, don't bother, if you're not fit you'll never come anywhere. And the tellers of trifle don't bother coming around this group."

He also includes the "runner." A runner is a gossiper who says, "I want you to pray for Mrs. So-and-so. I understand she and her husband had quite a fight last night, you know. Dear soul, I'm praying for her." Gossipers are not being honest. They're runners who disguise their running, gossiping under the false desire to pray for someone. The author goes on to say, "God knows to whom no petty thing is hidden, and all hearts speaketh and all hearts are open, all know where the runners are. The gossipers and the tattlers of tales, you let my book alone." How many of us possess the courage to be as honest and frank as he was?

He then talks about the "pincher." A pincher is someone who gives reluctantly. They hang on to their tithes as long as they can, pinching their money. The author says, "My intent was never to write such things unto them. Neither they nor any of these curious persons either lettered or unlettered." What does he mean by "these curious persons"? If a person's only interest concerning the deeper life is curiosity, whether they are ignorant or scholars, it does not make any difference. So many people can tell you about the deeper life in detail, but if you examine their life closely, they are not living it. Again he says, "I don't want any of these people reading what I have to say."

I respect this author, but I will contradict him here just a little bit. I am unwilling to withhold the open secret of spiritual power from those who can take it just because some cannot. And I'm not going to withhold the open secret of the victorious life from those who can understand it because of those who cannot understand.

In *The Cloud of Unknowing*, the author divides Christians into several categories. I will focus on the carnal Christian and the mature Christian. There may be other categories, but these two define the essence of spiritual maturity that I want to put forth. Understanding these two categories goes a long way toward solving the Christian maturity problem in our day.

I have been praying for years that there will be a sorting out in the Church, and I hope it is very soon. We have watered the truth down until the solution is so weak that if it were poison, it would not kill you, and if it were medicine, it would not cure you. It is just a diluted solution, and so we have weakened Christianity. I hope to live long enough to see a sorting out. I want to reach those who are not satisfied to be carnal Christians all their life, but who want by the grace of God to get past this business of telling trifles and gossiping and blaming themselves and others in jangling and pinching and being curious; those who want to go on unto the fullest measure, living by grace in this present life while still living in their mortal bodies.

If that has no appeal to you, and nothing is leaping up in your heart, trembling and saying, "Yes, Lord," then I do not know why you should continue in this study. But I think there will be some, and for those I am willing to spend my time and my life. Still, if you do not feel like that, if you think all this is just too much, and if you say to yourself, "Let's not get fanatical about this," then this study is not for you.

Is it fanatical to want to go on until you can perfectly love God, worthily praise God, and thus live in the will of God so that you are living in heaven while living on earth? If that is fanaticism, then it is the fanaticism of the law, the psalms, the prophets, and the New Testament. This fanaticism gave us the Friends of God who held close to the truth. This fanaticism also caused the birth of the Reformation.

These people in Church history were like worms in the soil, softening it up, getting it ready for the harvest, unseen but working with little groups here and there, who would not surrender to the common ways of the world. As angleworms and other types of worms live in the soil and move through it, the soil is kept soft and fixed so that rainwater can saturate it.

I therefore choose the lives of unremarkable, plain saints as examples, since they at least demonstrated the beginnings of Christian maturity. We do not know them or their names, but they salted down the nations—Germany, Holland, and the Latin countries—until the Reformation came. They had softened the soil in which to plant the seeds. Martin Luther could not have done what he did were it not for those who came before him, such as John Tyler and others like him who traveled up and down the land, preaching a new kind of Christian living. Together, they prepared the way for the Reformation.

Some will continue reading and listening, and others will not. Just like in Deuteronomy 9:23 when Israel came to Kadesh-barnea and turned back. "Likewise when the LORD sent you from Kadesh-barnea, saying, Go up and possess the land which I have given you; then ye rebelled against the commandment of the LORD your God, and ye believed him not, nor hearkened to his voice."

Israel refused to go over, turned around, and went back. Israel did not know they were sentencing themselves to forty years of aimless, useless wandering in the desert sands. They did not know it was a test and did not understand why they were taking it.

God did not say, "Now stand up here, everybody, breathe deep, for we will have a test." He let them make their own test, and they flubbed it. In this world of sin, flesh, and the devil, it is frightening and terrible that about 80–90 percent of the people whom God tested flunked the test.

However, not all did. Paul put it right when he said, "Wherefore he saith, Awake thou that sleepest, and arise from the dead, and Christ shall give thee light" (Ephesians 5:14). As Christians, we have the promise of God, and He has brought us to that place in which to experience His promise. For whatever reason, most of them turned their back on God's direction, and I am not sure why. They are slightly enticed to go forward, but their confidence in the leadership of God is in question.

I cannot imagine how Moses felt at that point when people turned back. Under God's leadership, he led the people of Israel out of Egypt and slavery to the place where they might cross into the Promised Land. Why would they refuse to go forward after their history of God faithfully leading them? Because they were more concerned about their past than they were about their future. They clung to their past and refused God's promise.

The author of *The Cloud of Unknowing* uses a phrase throughout the book that I find fascinating. "Look now forward and let be backward." Reading this for the first time, it is hard to understand what he means. However, I am sure Moses would have understood.

If your concept of the Christian life is part play, part social fun, and part religion, you will never go forward. You will shake your head, turn, and go backward. But if your concept of Christianity is that life is a battlefield, and this life is a preparation for a greater one, the cross of Jesus Christ is your symbol. You must carry it, die on it, rise, and live anew. Then you will move forward in your walk with Him. This will involve quite a bit of prayer on your part. Pray that God will help you to go forward and "let be backward." In *The Cloud of Unknowing*, the author believed that God knows better than we do, and that all we need to do is ask for His help. If we live in the past, God has nothing to do to help us along. How can anyone change the past? Yet if our focus is on the future, which is still a cloud to us, we will need God's help if we are to go forward.

Let us not worry about the past. Let us not look back to see what we might change or improve. While there's no way we can change the past, there *is* a way we can affect our future. The interesting thing about our future is that we do not know very much about it. Even our past becomes a little cloudy for us when we reflect back. But the future has aspects we cannot comprehend because they are rooted in eternity.

Nobody knows when exactly they are going to heaven, but in my own life, I want to focus on my path forward to spiritual maturity. I appreciate what Paul said: "Not as though I had already attained, either were already perfect . . ." (Philippians 3:12). If Paul can say this, then I can too. No matter my accomplishments, according to the apostle Paul, I have yet to attain perfection. By perfection he talks about full maturity and what God's will is for us.

Some people think of themselves as if perfect. They look back and see all the wonderful things they have accomplished in life and are quite proud of themselves. That was not Paul's attitude, however. No matter what he had accomplished in the past, he still had not "attained." Paul believed he had yet to accomplish in his life everything God wanted him to accomplish.

In the next phrase of Philippians 3:12, Paul says, ". . . but I follow after, if that I may apprehend that for which also I am apprehended of Christ Jesus." This was Paul's passion, to follow Christ no matter what it cost him. And it cost Paul everything, right down to his life.

In reading the epistles of the apostle Paul, you will find that he had an overwhelming, all-consuming passion for perfection. "I'm not perfect yet," Paul declares. And yet that was the goal and the direction of his life as a Christian. His idea of perfection did not come from the human side, but from God's side. Paul's hope of perfection was that he might be everything God wanted him to be, and where God wanted him to be.

Paul gave up everything, and his aim in life was Christian maturity in its utmost glory. I can almost hear the apostle Paul praying: *Cleanse the thoughts of my heart by the inspiration of Thy Holy Spirit, that I may perfectly love Thee and worthily praise Thee.*

God answered Paul's prayer. I, too, want to make this my daily prayer. I do not know what it means or what it will bring to my life. I am unsure what my Kadesh-barnea will be or if I will even recognize it, but through spiritual discipline my prayer shall be "Look now forward and let be backward."

In pursuing Christian maturity, I have come to the point where I refuse to tell God what to do or what not to do. When I was first saved, I sure had a lot of advice for God. I'm so grateful that He never listened to me along those lines. What a mess I would be in today if God did everything I asked of Him.

The apostle Paul's great challenge for Christians in his day and also in our day is to "grow in grace, and in the knowledge of our Lord and Saviour Jesus Christ" with no compromise. If I'm not growing in these two areas, I am not what God wants me to be or where God wants me to be. The challenge of Christian maturity is to let God be God and do His thing, whatever it is, in my life. God designs the path before us that will lead us to eternity with Him.

Heavenly Father, I praise Thee for Thy glorious impact on my life. Forgive me for the times I presumed to tell You what to do, and thank You for not doing what I tried to tell You. Amen.

SOFTLY AND TENDERLY
JESUS IS CALLING

Softly and tenderly Jesus is calling,
calling for you and for me;
see, on the portals he's waiting and watching,
watching for you and for me.

Come home, come home;
you who are weary come home;
earnestly, tenderly, Jesus is calling,
calling, O sinner, come home!

Why should we tarry when Jesus is pleading,.
pleading for you and for me?
Why should we linger and heed not his mercies,
mercies for you and for me?

Come home, come home;
you who are weary come home;
earnestly, tenderly, Jesus is calling,
calling, O sinner, come home!

Time is now fleeting, the moments are passing,
passing from you and from me;
shadows are gathering, deathbeds are coming,
coming for you and for me.

Come home, come home;
you who are weary come home;
earnestly, tenderly, Jesus is calling,
calling, O sinner, come home!

O for the wonderful love he has promised,
promised for you and for me!
Though we have sinned, he has mercy and pardon,
pardon for you and for me.

Will L. Thompson

3

THE OPPOSITION OF CHRISTIAN MATURITY

Brethren, I count not myself to have apprehended: but this one thing I do, forgetting those things which are behind, and reaching forth unto those things which are before, I press toward the mark for the prize of the high calling of God in Christ Jesus.

Philippians 3:13–14

The maturing Christian experiences a lot of opposition. And yet, as I think about it, I can understand why. It comes from without and within.

For those who think maturing and growing in Christ comes easily and naturally, let me share a verse from Proverbs 4:18: "But the path of the just is as the shining light, that shineth more and more unto the perfect day." In other words, the sun comes up when a person becomes a Christian, and the path of that Christian, as they move along, is like the rising of the dawn and the growing of the day, so that the light shines more and more unto the perfect day.

Christians seem to admire this verse. They quote it a great deal and even memorize it, but do they actually believe it? Many do not believe simply because they do not experience it, and what we do not experience, we have not truly believed. The majority of Christians remain where they are day after day, week after week, and the weeks turn into months, the months into years. The teenager moves into their twenties, their twenties soon turn into their thirties, and on and on. Revival meetings come and go, speakers come and go, and we have little spells when we hope to do better, but if we are being honest, we will agree that most Christians remain where they are until old age creeps up on them. And when you are old, you will not be one inch farther up the hill than when the sun first shone on you in conversion. I am not trying to deconvert, unchurch, or say you are not a Christian. I am merely pointing out that you stopped when you should have kept going.

What's worse, many Christians are now not as far advanced as they were only a few years ago. A few years ago, our faith was keener, our love warmer, our tears nearer the surface, our love of prayer greater, our purity and separation greater, and the principle within us more marked than it is now.

If that is true, then we are dealing with the carnal Christian. I am cautious about saying this because some people assert that God is no respecter of persons, and all Christians are alike. They say, "Are not all Christians justified? Are they not all regenerated? Are not all Christians members of

God's household and the body of Christ? Is not everything that they have in Christ theirs? Therefore, why do you make distinctions between Christians? All Christians are saints; we know from the Bible that they are all saints."

Yet if all Christians are alike and there is no distinction among them, then why did Christ talk of some producing fruit of thirtyfold, some sixtyfold, and some a hundredfold in the Christian life (Matthew 13:8; Luke 19:17)? Why did Jesus make such a distinction? Why did He say some would rule over many cities and others over a few cities, and some would have high positions and others not so high in the kingdom of God?

Why did Paul say there is no reason to be disturbed if we are not all alike? Why did he say, "I count all things but loss for the excellency of the knowledge of Christ Jesus my Lord: for whom I have suffered the loss of all things, and do count them but dung, that I may win Christ, and be found in him, not having mine own righteousness, which is of the law, but that which is through the faith of Christ, the righteousness which is of God by faith: that I may know him, and the power of his resurrection, and the fellowship of his sufferings, being made conformable unto his death; if by any means I might attain unto the resurrection of the dead" (Philippians 3:8–11)?

This kind of Christian can be defined by three different words. There is the carnal Christian, the common Christian, and the mediocre Christian. However, I will combine these three into one that I'll call *the carnal Christian*. And I do that because many Christians are born again, destined for heaven, but are trying to live their Christian life in the flesh. And that has brought a lot of problems into their life.

The carnal Christian believes in and carries around his Bible but is not distinguished by any spiritual superiority. They are just following customary and routine ways. I will leave it to you whether this describes you or not. Suppose you were simply a Christian of common quality or ability, not distinguished in any way that anybody would ever care to quote you or consult you about anything in particular. In that case, you are a common Christian, following customary ways, whatever they may be. That's my definition of the carnal Christian.

I don't care for the word *mediocre*, but it does describe many Christians. Many are mediocre in that they are but halfway up the peak. I don't mean halfway to heaven, but halfway to where they should be. They may no longer be wallowing in the valley, but they've not climbed to where the sun shines. Morally they are above the hardened sinner, though spiritually they remain in the shadows, away from the shining sun. That is where most Christians have settled.

Some Christians testified when they were young, "I'm not going to be mediocre. I will push my way up the mountain, until I become all I can be in this mortal life." But they have done little about it. If anything, they've lost ground. They are halfway Christians. Was that what Jesus meant when He said, "Because thou art lukewarm, and neither cold nor hot" (Revelation 3:16)?

Now, what does lukewarm mean? It means *tepid*—that is, neither cold nor hot, lacking in passion, lifeless—which is to say halfway up the peak, halfway up to where you could have been if you had pressed on.

If you turn and look back, you will find down the mountain that you are not in the valley, in the shadows and mists, but you're also not where you could have been. While morally above the hardened sinner, you are spiritually beneath the adoring saint, the mature Christian.

Is that the best Christ offers by His blood and by His heart in dying on the cross, by His resurrection from the dead, by His ascension to the right hand of the Father, by His sending forth of the Holy Spirit, by His inspiring the New Testament? Is this halfway Christian life the best that we can know?

Many mediocre, halfway believers and churches settle for just that. Does Jesus Christ expect that we should stop developing when we are only half-grown? Do we honor God by staying frozen in our development as though we are teenagers, or do we honor God by continuing to full Christian maturity? Is that what the Bible teaches, that God's people should quit and arrest their development and maturity?

Surely that is not what the Lord wants, and mediocrity does not agree with His teaching and the New Testament. Instead, we Christians must continue to grow, boldly moving forward into full maturity.

We must also understand that there will be opposition every step of the way. Again, though the devil cannot "un-save" me in any regard, he can keep me from moving forward in my Christian maturity. From what I know about the apostle Paul, he was vehement about not settling to be a mediocre Christian. He fought against being carnal in every aspect of his Christian life, and he knew he would face opposition daily in the form of the devil's attacks against him.

Paul makes this very clear when he writes to the Ephesian church, "Finally, my brethren, be strong in the Lord, and in the power of his might. Put on the whole armour of God, that ye may be able to stand against the wiles of the devil. For we wrestle not against flesh and blood, but against principalities, against powers, against the rulers of the darkness of this world, against spiritual wickedness in high places" (Ephesians 6:10–12).

He reminds us that we are facing a battle, and we have a responsibility before God to prepare ourselves for this battle. This is where Christian maturity comes in. As we grow in the grace and knowledge of the Lord Jesus Christ, we become more equipped to face the battles before us. If you have yet to encounter a battle, something is wrong. If you are not on the battlefield, you are not where God wants you to be.

In the Old Testament, David was fully prepared to face Goliath. Consider his conversation with King Saul: "And Saul said to David, Thou art not able to go against this Philistine to fight with him: for thou art but a youth, and he a man of war from his youth. And David said unto Saul, Thy servant kept his father's sheep, and there came a lion, and a bear, and took a lamb out of the flock: And I went out after him, and smote him, and delivered it out of his mouth: and when he arose against me, I caught him by his beard, and smote him, and slew him. Thy servant slew both the lion and the bear: and this uncircumcised Philistine shall be as one of them, seeing he hath defied the armies of the living God. David said moreover, The LORD that delivered me out of the paw of the lion, and out of the paw of the bear, he will deliver me out of the hand of this Philistine. And Saul said unto David, Go, and the LORD be with thee" (1 Samuel 17:33–37).

At first glance it may be hard to see how all this prepared David for such a one as Goliath. But what David learned is that God knows what He is doing. We are strengthened through battles, both big and small. Follow God in the path He has set forth by His Spirit.

The carnal Christians do not understand this. When they face difficulty, they back away as much as possible. Whatever undermines their happiness at some point is their enemy, or so they think. The carnal Christian lives for fleshly endeavors. Whatever the flesh can do is what the carnal Christian wants to do. Anything to please the flesh is their focus.

The more I grow in my Christian experience, the more I recognize the battles before me. When I first became a Christian, I thought all my problems were over. I thought all I needed to do was wait until I was transported into heaven. If anything challenged that, I ran from it as quickly as possible.

Paul testified that he had not yet arrived, and there were still battles for him to face. If that was true with the apostle Paul, why do you think it is not true for us today? He was so dedicated to his Christian maturity that he did not allow anything to get in the way or slow him down. This is why Paul said, "Let us therefore, as many as be perfect, be thus minded" (Philippians 3:15). If we are to leave the carnal Christian environment behind us, we must take to heart the perfection Paul is talking about here. Perfection means complete maturity from God's perspective, not ours. And our enemy is anything that opposes our Christian development and maturity. We need God's help in recognizing that enemy and understanding how, by His grace, we can overcome any and all opposition.

It's not hard to understand why the devil is opposed to Christians growing in the grace and knowledge of Jesus Christ. He hates spiritual maturity and will do anything to get us to compromise and settle for mediocrity in our lives. We can see the results of his attacks in churches today.

In many churches, Christians are trying to keep the difficult side of Christianity away from them. They are trying to present a gospel without roots in the Bible, which is easy and fun and does not offend anybody. After all, God loves everybody. (I am tired of hearing that because it is often taken out of context.) It seems the gospel preached today is not offensive to anybody, no matter their lifestyle, so that anybody can readily accept it.

I have discovered, however, that each opposition I face head-on is another step forward in my Christian maturity. Getting over the opposition puts me where God wants me to be and defeats the enemy. It allows me to graduate to the next level of maturity.

In Thy grace, O God, I choose to live. As I dwell in Thy grace, my knowledge and love of Christ grows continually. I praise You, Father, for helping me to press on toward maturity, day by day. Amen.

A Mighty Fortress
Is Our God

A mighty fortress is our God,
a bulwark never failing;
our helper he, amid the flood
of mortal ills prevailing.
For still our ancient foe
does seek to work us woe;
his craft and power are great,
and armed with cruel hate,
on earth is not his equal.

Did we in our own strength confide,
our striving would be losing,
were not the right Man on our side,
the Man of God's own choosing.
You ask who that may be?
Christ Jesus, it is he;
Lord Sabaoth his name,
from age to age the same;
and he must win the battle.

And though this world, with devils filled,
should threaten to undo us,
we will not fear, for God has willed
his truth to triumph through us.
The prince of darkness grim,
we tremble not for him;
his rage we can endure,
for lo! his doom is sure;
one little word shall fell him.

That Word above all earthly powers
no thanks to them abideth;

the Spirit and the gifts are ours
through him who with us sideth.
Let goods and kindred go,
this mortal life also;
the body they may kill:
God's truth abideth still;
his kingdom is forever!

Martin Luther

4

THE ENEMY
OF CHRISTIAN MATURITY

The enemy that sowed them is the devil; the harvest is the
end of the world; and the reapers are the angels.

Matthew 13:39

I need to respond to why there are so many carnal Christians—
those who have settled for a little fun or something to tickle
and charm the fancy of the carnality crowd. Carnal Christians, when hearing the Lord's call to take up their cross and
follow Him up toward the heights, bargain with the Lord
like hucksters. They grumble and haggle and try to negotiate with Him.

Whenever we see the finger of God pointing or beckoning,
or after we read about the life of some great saint, we are left
aglow with the desire to clamber up the mountain and be a
Christian as near to spiritual perfection as we can be in this

life. But instead of going, many of us waver. We begin asking questions, and we attempt to bargain with God.

In *The Merchant of Venice*, Shakespeare said of a certain fellow, "God made him, and therefore let him pass for a man." But we who are Christians have been born again, we have the Life, and the root of the matter is within us. Too often, however, when the Lord calls us to the heights, we begin to negotiate and ask, "What will it cost me? O Lord, I want to go, but what will it cost me?"

Anyone who brings up the question of consequence in the Christian life is a carnal Christian, for there is one thing the mature Christian never asks concerning the cross. Jesus said, "And when he had called the people unto him with his disciples also, he said unto them, Whosoever will come after me, let him deny himself, and take up his cross, and follow me" (Mark 8:34). Whoever takes up the cross never asks what the consequence will be because everyone knows the consequence of crucifixion.

When it comes to the subject of the deeper life, some might say, "I'm interested in this deeper-life business, and I agree with the preacher, but what will it cost me over time?" You become something of a religious huckster when you ask questions like that. Also, "What will it cost me in terms of money? How much of my money will I have to give away? After all, I have been tithing." I'm quite sure that most mediocre Christians are tithing.

The negotiating goes on: "What will it cost me in labor? What will it cost me in friendships? Will I have to give up a friendship that's dear to me?" I'm not scorning friendships. It is wonderful and lovely to have good friends, and such relationships will carry over into the world to come. But if we hesitate about our friends when Christ tells us to follow Him, we're not worthy of being among the saints. Instead, we've settled to be carnal, mediocre Christians, halfway to the peak, stuck on the ascent. I may not be a hardened sinner, but I'm certainly not a shining saint when I ask, "What will it cost me?"

Such teachings seem rather harsh and challenging, but I am actually softening the language a bit compared to the Lord's words on this subject, particularly in the book of Matthew, chapter 16: "Then said Jesus unto his disciples, If any man will come after me, let him deny himself, and take up his cross, and follow me. For whosoever will save his life shall lose it: and whosoever will lose his life for my sake shall find it" (24–25).

If we are going to advance in our Christian maturity, it will be at our inconvenience. All spiritual advances must be made at personal inconvenience. If it does not inconvenience you, there is no cross in it. If it costs you nothing, and there's no disturbance, bother, or element of sacrifice, you're getting nowhere. Rather, you have stopped and pitched your tent halfway between the lowland and the peak. We must ask ourselves, "Was there ever a convenient cross? Was there ever found a convenient way to die?" I, for one, have never heard of any such way.

To understand the Bible, we have to conclude that judgment will not be convenient, yet we constantly search around for convenience. But mountain climbers are always in peril, and making their way upward to the summit is an inconvenience.

Another obstacle that gets in the way when we hear the voice of Jesus calling us is fun. Yet no one who asks, "Will it be fun?" will ever be anything but a carnal Christian. They will remain mediocre until death comes for them and will never be known as having much of any spiritual qualities or gifts of the Holy Spirit. They will not come to know the Lord in a deep and personal way.

Why do so many halfway-to-the peak Christians demand that the Christian life be fun? Perhaps because whole organizations have been established to give it to them, organizations committed to mixing Christianity with fun for our young people. Of course, the young are just as responsible before God as older people. The teenager who meets Jesus and is converted is just as responsible for the inconvenience, the cost, and all the rest as someone of seventy is. Christ never offered amusement or entertainment, and yet many feel they have to provide such things if we are to draw people nowadays to become interested in Christianity. These ones are carnal Christians.

Yet another question that carnal Christians ask when negotiating with God is, "Is it popular? Are others doing this, too?" They seek the group's approval and so try to form solidarity to bolster each other's staggering courage. But the mature Christian never asks, "Is it popular?" Rather, the mature Christian asks, "Is it the will of God?" That is the only thing they are concerned about.

Heaven is where the will of God is always done. Hell is where the will of God is unknown, except for the judgment that sent people there. In between heaven, where the will of God is perfectly done, and hell, where it will never be done, is a group of people trying to decide whether they want God's will. When they ask if it's popular, they are avoiding the pain of standing alone. Some cannot muster what it takes to stand alone.

In other words, the mark of mediocrity and the carnal Christian is a list of questions they ask: "God, if I go on, what will it cost me? Will it be safe if I go on? Will it be convenient? Will there be any fun in it? Will I have to stand alone?"

Remember, our motto is "Look now forward and let be backward." Someone once asked me, "You said that open praisers or blamers of themselves were in no position to hear the call of God. What do you mean by a blamer of myself?" Well, one of the slick tricks of the devil is to try to bog you down by discouraging you, and he does this by getting you to look back at yourself and by accusing you of being a hypocrite. Sure, you were a religious huckster back then. Suppose you negotiated with God in that ignoble manner when He called you to take up your cross and follow Him. You lived the Christian life according to your convenience, or you looked to what was easy, fun, or popular before answering His call. Suppose all that is true. Is that going to stop you now from moving upward to the heights? Is it going to prevent you from following Him faithfully?

If you are discouraged by this description of a carnal Christian, I would ask you not to be. We must stop thinking or worrying about ourselves altogether. We must "look now forward and let be backward." For if you go back and beat yourself up like the one who flagellates himself until he bleeds, showing how spiritual you are by confessing that you are no good, you will just be fussing with yourself and not getting anywhere spiritually. No Christian will cover much distance until they lift their eyes to Him and His cross and stop focusing on themselves. Human eyes were made to look out, not in. But God created us to look out, not back in.

Rather than being introspective, we are to be prospective. Prospect means looking forward, not backward. So let us not look back. Confession is necessary and good if done in the right way. A man with a big, friendly smile once said to me, "I tried confession for a while and gave it up because I could never find all my sins." There is an honest man for you. He could never get to where it ended. Go back and dig up everything wrong with you; you will find yourself going around in circles. The more you dig, the more you will harm yourself. It is like operating on yourself.

Our God is the God of new beginnings. The burden of our past is removed from the Christian's back and left rolling down the mountainside. From that point on, we look forward and not backward. Looking back at your mistakes—the sins you committed, your ignoble mediocrity, how common you have been, and how undistinguished your spiritual life is—will make you like an immovable rock halfway up the mountain. The thing to do is stop blaming yourself. Stop praising others too, as one is just as bad as the other.

A man who boasts is no better and no worse than the man who always blames himself. We don't need to be warned against praising ourselves, because that sin is not so hard to recognize. We often find it easy to get victory over this form of pride. But it's not so easy to get victory over the blaming of ourselves.

We can be comforted, however, in that He understands our situation. If you were to take yourself apart until every grain of dust from which you are made was lying in the open before the eyes of God, you would not be telling God anything new, because He knows you are but dust. If you were to go back in your life and dig up every memory, every shameful act or thought, you would not reveal anything new to Him. God knows all about everything and, being merciful, He stands ready to forgive. "As far as the east is from the west, so far hath he removed our transgressions from us. Like as a father pitieth his children, so the LORD pitieth them that fear him." Sweet Psalm 103, I thank the Lord it was written. "For he knoweth our frame; he remembereth that we are dust."

So far we've been describing the carnal Christian. Next, I want to tell you what the carnal Christian can do about their situation.

I thank Thee, O God, for Your faithfulness in forgetting all my past sins. Help me as I repent and go forward in my walk with Thee. Amen.

HE HIDETH MY SOUL

A wonderful Savior is Jesus my Lord,
a wonderful Savior to me.
He hideth my soul in the cleft of the rock,
where rivers of pleasure I see.

He hideth my soul in the cleft of the rock
that shadows a dry, thirsty land.
He hideth my life in the depths of his love,
and covers me there with his hand,
and covers me there with his hand.

A wonderful Savior is Jesus my Lord;
he taketh my burden away.

49

He holdeth me up, and I shall not be moved;
he giveth me strength as my day.

He hideth my soul in the cleft of the rock
that shadows a dry, thirsty land.
He hideth my life in the depths of his love,
and covers me there with his hand,
and covers me there with his hand.

With numberless blessings each moment he crowns,
and filled with his fullness divine,
I sing in my rapture, "Oh, glory to God
for such a Redeemer as mine!"

He hideth my soul in the cleft of the rock
that shadows a dry, thirsty land.
He hideth my life in the depths of his love,
and covers me there with his hand,
and covers me there with his hand.

When clothed in his brightness, transported I rise
to meet him in clouds of the sky,
his perfect salvation, his wonderful love,
I'll shout with the millions on high.

He hideth my soul in the cleft of the rock
that shadows a dry, thirsty land.
He hideth my life in the depths of his love,
and covers me there with his hand,
and covers me there with his hand.

Fanny Crosby

5

THE GROWTH
OF CHRISTIAN MATURITY

I am crucified with Christ: nevertheless I live; yet not I, but Christ liveth in me: and the life which I now live in the flesh I live by the faith of the Son of God, who loved me, and gave himself for me.

Galatians 2:20

Many of God's people wallow in carnal Christianity all their life. For some reason, they do not know there is a choice to go forward in their Christian experience. It is not because they do not know what the Bible says, but rather because they have not personally experienced the truth in the Word of God.

Because we can quote a text, we assume we have the experience of that text. This, to my mind, is one of the greatest hindrances to spiritual progress and one of the deadliest, most chilling breezes that ever blew across the Church. This strange textualism assumes that because we can quote a verse, we have the content of that verse inside us and are living it.

I can walk around First National Bank and even enter the building, but I do not own one red penny in First National Bank. My experience with that bank is superficial. That can also be said of our experience with the Word of God. I can look up and memorize verses but not truly internalize any of the things I have memorized.

We look at the above text and rejoice that "Christ liveth in me." We are so ever thankful that Christ lives in us, and we long for when He will come and receive us into His presence. This was the great passion of King David in the Old Testament when he wrote, "As the hart panteth after the water brooks, so panteth my soul after thee, O God. My soul thirsteth for God, for the living God: when shall I come and appear before God?" (Psalm 42:1–2).

This passion in David should be in every Christian today. If I am to grow out of carnal Christianity, I will need a passion equal to the task. David had that passion. But do I truly? Sadly, many are strangers to this kind of passion, which is why there are so many carnal Christians in today's Church.

Some Christians will not understand this or will feel disappointed. Some may get to the point where they say, "What's the use?" They need help understanding the subject because the Creed of Contentment has stopped them.

The Creed of Contentment says that you are complete in Christ; therefore, be glad because nothing else can be done for you, and any effort to get ahead and improve is put down as fanaticism. It is ironic that over the past years, the

New Testament, particularly the book of Romans that talks about Christ's finished work in us, has been so expounded that many Christians have stopped dead in their tracks—no more forward motion. They have met some truth they will not obey. The Lord will positively not quibble over any truth you will not obey. But if you do not obey it—if you stop somewhere, if there's something you refuse to do, some confession you won't make, some straightening out that you won't cooperate with, some act of obedience you will not submit to—then you will be brought to a halt. There is no going on from there, and people sitting around in the Church are saved but are not moving forward. They are saved but wallow in carnality.

They have trusted Christ and believe their sins are forgiven, but something has stopped them from going forward in their spiritual growth. Many have heard good preaching, but it has not meant much because that truth was stopped by non-obedience.

Another reason why carnal Christians do not move forward is that they have accepted a state of chronic discouragement as the normal condition for a Christian. They are believers, but not for themselves. They say, "It's only for others. I believe in this life—this progressive, victorious Christian life—but it can't be for me." They have been to the altar several times and attended Bible conferences and done all the right things, but they got into a chronic discouragement and can't seem to get out.

I see this in many of the churches I visit. Unbelief and discouragement say, "Yes, I believe what you're saying is for somebody else, but not for me; some other time, but not now; some other place, but not here." Some view that as modesty and meekness, but it is neither modesty nor meekness; it is discouragement resulting from unbelief.

Many people will read *The Cloud of Unknowing* with great satisfaction. Their attitude is that it was for people six-hundred-plus years ago, but not for them. The book was written for that particular time and place, but not for today, not for here. Without realizing it, they are languishing in a state of chronic discouragement, like someone who's been sick for so long that they don't believe they can become well again.

When Jesus saw the man lying by the pool, He asked, "Wilt thou be made whole?" (John 5:6). Why did Jesus say that to him? He never said it to anybody else in the New Testament. Wouldn't any person suffering with an illness want to be made well? Only up to a certain point does the average person want to get well, for after living with a chronic illness for so long, it becomes a part of them. They don't want to lose it because they wouldn't have anything to talk about afterward. They feel they are martyrs and pity themselves and feel it's their cross to bear, and so they don't want to get well. They say they do but have learned to live with their chronic sickness without expecting any change.

If they've had their sickness for over twenty years and it hasn't killed them yet, they figure they can last another twenty years, so they don't try to get well. Jesus made this man whole again because he *wanted* to be made whole. Jesus may have passed him by had the man exhibited a chronic state of discouragement.

This chronic discouragement is why some Christians remain in carnal Christianity and never progress in their spiritual life. Some do not even desire to go forward. David's heart, on the other hand, was to get well, to grow ever closer to God. "As the hart panteth after the water brooks, so panteth my soul after thee, O God." David had an overwhelming passion for the water brooks. He thirsted for the Living Water of God, and nothing else could satisfy him. He recognized his thirst, but more important, he recognized what would satiate that thirst, and nothing else mattered.

If we are satisfied with where we are, we will never move one step further. To look forward and go forward, we must be willing to rise above our chronic discouragement and, with God's help, press onward regardless of the consequences.

Another reason so many carnal Christians stay at this level of Christianity is because they have accepted the cult of respectability. They have chosen to be cool, proper, self-possessed, well-rounded, or *adjusted*. It seems everybody is coming at you with a screwdriver, trying to adjust you. We go to school to adjust, for we ought to become adjusted. We bring psychiatry into the Church, hiring professionals with psychological screwdrivers to adjust people. Everybody seeks to be properly adjusted, broad in their outlook and always poised, as nobody wants to be thought a fanatic.

Carnal Christians have forgotten that every superior soul from Christ on down to today was initially considered a fanatic, overzealous, even deranged. We sing the hymns of Charles and John Wesley and talk about them as if they were saints, which indeed they were. When John Wesley lived, he could not keep a decent suit clean for the eggs thrown at him. The founder of the Methodists was a learned Oxford man, yet he was such a fiery apostle that people would throw eggs and rocks at him. He would come home all banged up after preaching his sermon. He wore a long tailcoat and pin-striped pants, and his hair was neatly combed when he went out. But when he returned, he needed both a tailor and a barber. He was considered a little off because of the spiritual progress he was making.

I do not mean we should deliberately become a nuisance in our society. Plenty of other people are doing that. But if we live out our commitment to Jesus Christ and allow Him to live in us and through us, we will become a genuine threat to the way society functions. And if we think as Christians we can blend in with the culture, we have yet to understand the New Testament.

Nobody wants to be thought of as extreme, especially with regard to religious matters, which is why so many are converted but stop growing right there. Thank God there are a few the Bible talks about as being different from that. Revelation 3:4 says, "Thou hast a few names even in Sardis which have not defiled their garments; and they shall walk with me in white: for they are worthy." Thus some people were sufficiently different, even during times of backsliding and general coldness of heart. They walked with Him in white and were considered worthy.

It is rather suspicious that the carnal Christian blends in with society and the culture; some you cannot tell from the rest of the world. This is not what Christianity is all about.

Some might ask, "Are you trying to whip up a desire in our hearts?" No, I am not trying to whip up a desire, because I know better. I realize I cannot put a desire in your heart. Again, listen to the author of *The Cloud of Unknowing*:

"Our Lord had of his great mercy called thee and led thee on to him." So then, are you prepared to say that our Lord of His great mercy has called and led you on to Him? Only God through the Holy Spirit can create such a desire in one's heart. It will last for only a little while if it is created by anybody or anything else and will eventually peter out. I cannot even stir up the desire in my own heart; rather, I need to yield to the Holy Spirit as I pray over the Word of God.

We must understand that it is God who plants the desire in our hearts, and He is always previous to anything we do. If you have any desire at all for God, it is because He graciously put that desire in your heart. If that does not describe us, then we're living in a state of carnal Christianity.

Do you remember a time when you did not exist? I do not remember such a time. Nevertheless, there was a time when I was not, and by the everlasting love of the Godhead, He made me. In other words, God was there previously, and out of His love and for His glory, God made me when I was not.

Then He bought me with the price of His Son's precious blood when I was lost. Once more, God preceded me; He was previous. Thus I believe in prevenient grace. I do not believe a person can ever be nudged, pushed, or jostled into the deeper life in the kingdom of God—that is, except by the Holy Spirit. God made you out of nothing into a human being and breathed into you the breath of life, and you became a living soul when you were nothing but a zero out in vacuity and emptiness. And He did that out of the everlasting love of His Godhead.

As a carnal Christian, if you are going to get out of that stagnant place, it has to be in following God and allowing Him to be Lord in your life. Too many times we want to be

God, like Lucifer who said, "I will be like the most High" (Isaiah 14:14). When we surrender to God and allow Him to be who He is, we begin to see things change in our attitude and heart. We begin to hunger and thirst for something we do not have. That is the way out of this spiritual stagnancy.

O Father, You have poured a desire for Thyself into my heart. I will not reject that desire. I will cultivate it and allow it to be the passion of my heart. Every moment of every day I yield to Thee and Thy Word. Amen.

THE FIRM FOUNDATION

How firm a foundation, ye saints of the Lord,
is laid for your faith in God's excellent Word!
What more can be said than to you God hath said,
to you who for refuge to Jesus have fled?

Fear not, I am with thee, O be not dismayed,
for I am thy God, and will still give thee aid;
I'll strengthen thee, help thee, and cause thee to stand,
upheld by my righteous, omnipotent hand.

When through the deep waters I call thee to go,
the rivers of sorrow shall not overflow;
for I will be near thee, thy troubles to bless,
and sanctify to thee thy deepest distress.

When through fiery trials thy pathway shall lie,
my grace, all sufficient, shall be thy supply;
the flame shall not hurt thee; I only design
thy dross to consume, and thy gold to refine.

The soul that on Jesus hath leaned for repose,
I will not, I will not desert to its foes;
that soul, though all hell should endeavor to shake,
I'll never, no, never, no, never forsake.

Robert Keen

6

THE INWARD PASSION FOR
CHRISTIAN MATURITY

For it is God which worketh in you both to will and to do
of his good pleasure.

Philippians 2:13

For the Christian, spiritual passion is essential and cannot be imitated. It must be real, or it does not last long. I
cannot create this passion in my life, and I cannot create
it in somebody else's life. Also, I am not in control of this
inward passion for Christian maturity. When I understand
this, I am one step further in my journey toward growing
in the Lord.

If, however, you don't have a longing after God, if you accepted the common state of living and are not engaged in any
ongoing spiritual journey, and if God hasn't by His love and

mercy kindled within you the fire of desire and drawn you to himself, you will not progress spiritually. You are stagnant.

All spiritual adventures were internal before they became external. The fire of desire for God must be inward before it can become outward, and the outward flowing is only secondary. A study of the saints and heroes of the faith will show that this desire all occurred inside them before it flowed outside.

For those who want to go forward in their Christian maturity, I want to give you some of what the author of *The Cloud of Unknowing* meant when he said, "Look up now, weak wretch, and see what thou art. What art thou, and what hast thou merited, thus to be called of our Lord?" You may feel you have come to amount to something. You've studied the Scriptures and can read the New Testament in Greek. Isn't that wonderful, you wretch? But what are you? What have you merited?

The author goes on to say, "What weary wretched heart, and sleeping in sloth, is that, the which is not wakened with the draught of this love and the voice of this calling!" How long have you been a common Christian, measuring yourself by others, judging yourself by others, and thanking the Lord that you are converted?

If God has given you this inward passion for following Him, for growing in Him, then get up and say, "God, if you lead me by the Scriptures and by the Spirit, I'll go forward. I've hung around here and have heard you talk of drought long enough in this place, 'Get thee up and go into a land which I will show thee.'"

I hope you've heard that calling, heard God graciously leading you onward. He has chosen you to be one of His special people and then set you in the place of new pastures where He says, "Thou mayest be fed with the sweetness of his love."

⁂

The Church's challenge today is getting that which we already have in Christ into us, yet it is something we're not doing much about. But we can begin by looking not to the past but to what lies ahead. If we are going to get to new places where we haven't been before, not where we have been, we ought not start by speaking of what God has done for us. Instead, we should start by looking at what He hasn't done for us yet because we wouldn't let Him.

We have many examples of great saints who had such a desire and longing for God that nothing stopped them from pressing forward into Christian maturity. What, then, is the real problem here? Why can't we move on in our Christian maturity? Is it that we are always looking backward? I think it's wonderful to reflect back and thank God for all the blessings He has bestowed on us in our lives, all the prayers He has answered. Yet we need to set our hearts on looking forward in the direction God wants us to go. In front of us lies our Kadesh-barnea.

Why is it so many Christians do not have this burning desire within them, this longing for God? It's simply because we won't let God give it to us. It only comes to you by the hand of God with your consent. God says, "I'm ready to pour a little liquid fire into your heart." We respond, "No, Lord, for that would make me strange. I'd be seen as fanatical, and I'd have to give up some things." We want His heaven, the benefits of His cross, and the bridge over hell, but we won't let Him kindle a deeper love of Him, the desire for more of Him. So, if you come to have this passion and desire, it will be by the hand of God and by your consent.

Christian maturity is not something we do in ourselves, it's something we let God do in us. What would happen in your spiritual life if you were to let God alone and stopped preventing Him from doing what He wants to do? What is it God wants? His will is to kindle your heart with a special longing after Him, to bless you and lead you out of the common carnal state where most Christians remain stuck. To do this, I recommend spending an uninterrupted hour with God daily—not an hour in Bible study, but an hour looking up to God, communing with Him. Here is a beautiful truth: God desires you more than you could ever desire Him. If we give God what He wants along this line, we will find our hearts full of an overwhelming desire and longing for God himself. Our longing will not be for what God can do, but for what and who God is.

As you practice this spiritual discipline before God, do not forget that any longing you have comes from Him; it isn't yours, and you have no right to claim it. If you find you don't have any real longing, it is because you're holding back, keeping Him from putting it in your heart by His hand once you consent and submit to His will for you. After you consent, He will kindle your heart as you look to Him and let Him alone. You don't have to coax God. Isn't it wonderful to know we don't have to get on our knees and beg Him like a reluctant father is begged by his child?

God is ready to do His great work in you, and He abides with us. All you have to do is consent to it, then press on in faith and trust. He wants you to mature in your Christian life and relationship with Him, so look to Him in full surrender and let Him alone.

Of course, looking to God and letting Him alone isn't how most Americans do it. Americans are born do-it-yourselfers. We prefer to get our fingers on everything, which is the way many Christians tend. We believe God does the hard work but is glad to have us along to help out. But that is *not* how God works in our lives. We must adopt the motto of looking to God and letting Him alone. Leave your hands down at your sides and stop trying to tell God what to do. He's the physician, you're the patient.

"It is God which worketh in you" (Philippians 2:13), but to do what? We don't know, but we need to trust in His love for us. If we would only let God do what He wants and not offer Him our advice or help but instead submit to His authority once and for all, He then will do His mighty work in us.

I can be very religious, passionate about rituals, Bible study, and going to church, but that is no substitute for a passion for the person of God. For I need to know God as He wants me to know Him. It is one thing to know aspects of God—every religion in the world shares some of that knowledge—but it's something else entirely to know Him intimately, to have a passion for God himself. Many want to know God just so they can get from Him what they want. This is religious manipulation, and it leaves them with no access to God.

We must ask ourselves whether our prayer life is based on a genuine longing for God, or is our prayer life mostly about bargaining with God to do something in our life or someone else's life that maybe God isn't interested in doing?

Our prayer life is like a checkup where we assess our relationship with Him and our understanding of His will. Are we praying according to the will of God?

Put the focus on God himself. Open your heart and let God do what He wants with your uncompromising permission. When we yield to the desire to know God more intimately, our passion is kindled by His hand, and we begin to understand God's will and what He wants to do in our hearts.

God does not want to make me an influential celebrity. God does not need celebrities, and in fact they get in the way of God's glory. David said of God, "For every beast of the forest is mine, and the cattle upon a thousand hills" (Psalm 50:10). What does any person have that God wants or needs? Nothing. Like Lucifer, we demand to be God and establish the conditions of our relationship; we are the ones who tell God what to do and when to do it.

My having a longing and a passion for God himself is sure to overcome all of that nonsense. I shouldn't be as interested in what God can do for me as in how God reveals himself to me according to the Word of God and His will. God's "good pleasure" is of supreme importance here. Is my life a reflection of this pleasure of God, or is my life a reflection of my pleasure?

One of the most exciting things about being a follower of Christ is to discover something new about God in my life. A person who has been a minister as long as I have and a Christian as long as I have should know everything there is to know about God. But I will be the first to tell you this is not so, at least with me.

Occasionally, God reveals something about himself I didn't know before, feeding my hunger and desire for Him. And so I go on in my pursuit of God and my everyday walk with Him.

At this point, I want to stress that Christian maturity begins in this life but flows over into our life in heaven with Him. What God is doing in my life and the passions and desires He is giving me are centered on eternity. We don't know what heaven is going to be like, but we need to understand that God is preparing us for His kingdom. Every day we are becoming more prepared. We "grow in grace, and in the knowledge of our Lord and Saviour Jesus Christ" (2 Peter 3:18). God's work in us is to reveal His will and good pleasure, helping us to go forward in our Christian maturity with our eyes fixed on Him alone.

O God, as the hart pants after the water brooks, so pants my heart after Thee. I desire Thee and only Thee. I will surrender all for the knowledge of Thee. Amen.

MY GOD, HOW WONDERFUL THOU ART

My God, how wonderful Thou art,
Thy majesty how bright,
How beautiful Thy mercy seat,
in depths of burning light!

How dread are Thine eternal years,
O everlasting LORD;

67

by prostrate spirits, day and night,
incessantly adored.

How wonderful, how beautiful,
the sight of Thee must be,
Thine endless wisdom, boundless pow'r,
and awful purity.

O how I fear Thee, Living God,
with deepest, tend'rest fears,
and worship Thee with trembling hope,
and penitential tears.

Yet I may love Thee too, O LORD,
Almighty as Thou art;
for Thou hast stooped to ask of me
the love of my poor heart.

No earthly father loves like Thee,
no mother e'er so mild,
bears and forbears, as Thou hast done
with me, Thy sinful child.

Father of Jesus, love's reward,
what rapture will it be,
prostrate before Thy throne to lie,
and ever gaze on Thee!

Frederick William Faber

7

THE PRICE OF
CHRISTIAN MATURITY

That I may know him, and the power of his resurrection,
and the fellowship of his sufferings, being made conformable unto his death.

Philippians 3:10

To grow in Christian maturity is to experience the Lord Jesus
Christ in our personal life. We must seek to know Him as
fully as He can be known and as He desires to be known.
When Paul said, "That I may know him," the word *know*
means to be acquainted with Him, but it also means to experience Him. You can be acquainted with someone and yet
not have experienced that person in any real sense.

If I introduced you to a friend of mine, you could then
say, "Yes, I'm acquainted with him." But you have not experienced him in the sense that I have after spending time

with him, traveling with him, preaching with him, talking with him countless times, and praying with him. To become acquainted with God is one thing, but to go on to experience God in His richness and unfailing love is something far more.

The apostle Paul expressed "I want to know him" in that depth and rich intensity of experience, as personality cannot be fully known by one encounter. You may meet a person you do not particularly like at first, but after you get to know them, you come to like them because you saw the hidden potential in their personality you didn't know existed before. The same is true with Christ, who can increase the intimacy of experience unlike any other personality.

A grave oversight among a lot of Christians today is not only do they not seek to know Christ in the rich intimacy of experience, but they are not even talking about it in their churches. The yearning to know Him in increasing measure seems to be missing. Yet as we experience Jesus more and more, we begin to discover unexpected things about Him. For example, in Scripture He's often referred to as "that." Somebody may ask, "But if Jesus Christ is a person, why do you call him 'that'?" As Paul himself says, "God will reveal even that unto you if you think otherwise." Before we can know God as He or Him, we first must come to know God as *that*.

Remember what the angel said to Mary? "And the angel answered and said unto her, The Holy Ghost shall come upon thee, and the power of the Highest shall overshadow thee: therefore also that holy thing which shall be born of thee shall be called the Son of God" (Luke 1:35). "That holy thing."

The apostle John, the man who laid his head upon the breast of Jesus, begins his wondrous first epistle with the word *that*: "That which was from the beginning, which we have heard, which we have seen with our eyes, which we have looked upon, and our hands have handled, of the Word of life" (1 John 1:1). Personality is not found there yet. It's not until the last two lines of the third stanza that John brings in personality.

Jesus Christ, while a person and the Son of the living God, is also the source of everything; He is the foundation of everything you and I have been created to enjoy (Colossians 1:15–20). He is the fountain of all truth, and even more, He is truth itself. He is the source and spring of all beauty, and even more, He is beauty itself. He is the source of all love, and even more, He is love itself. He is the fountain of all wisdom, and even more, He is wisdom itself, as all the treasures of wisdom and knowledge are hidden away in Him. He is the fountain of all goodness, the source of all life, and yet He is much more than that. He said, "I am the bread of life." As Robert Robinson's song tells us, he is the brightness of the Father's glory, the sunshine of the Father's face.

What did Jesus mean when He said, "Thou hast left thy first love" (Revelation 2:4)? He didn't mean one's first love consecutively in the sense that there's love number one and love number two and love number three. He meant we left our first *degree* of love. I'm trying to bring about in the Church a rediscovery of the loveliness of the Savior, so that we might begin to love Him again with an intensity of love such as our fathers knew, to restore that love in our lives.

When Abraham saw the city with foundations whose builder and maker is God, he would not build a house after that. He said, "I'll never try to imitate it. I'll live in a tent till I get my house up there. It was so beautiful." In the book of Hebrews, it says, "For he looked for a city which hath foundations, whose builder and maker is God" (Hebrews 11:10). Earth's fairest beauty and heaven's brightest splendor are enfolded in Jesus Christ. When we begin to understand that, we see that everything in this world pales in comparison. Abraham discovered that no matter how much a person spends building a palace down here, it would never compare with what God had in store for him in heaven.

That brings me to the thought that it costs to know Jesus Christ like this. Most people will not pay the price for it. That is why so many stay at the level of carnal Christianity. They think they're growing simply because they have given up their evil activities—the grossly sinful things that are injurious and unclean. And so they avoid unholy places and behaviors. But if that's all there is, it is still the mark of the carnal, mediocre Christian who has never pressed on to maturity. There's much more to spiritual maturity than what we once did in the past.

We see in the life of the apostle Paul that he surrendered both the bad and the good. He said not only the bad things did he have to give up, but also what things were gain for him, those he counted as loss for Christ (Philippians 3:7–9). The things that were gain for him and that he had every legal and moral right to declare, "This is mine, and Christianity is not going to take it from me." He went on to say, "I've given up even that because I've seen something so much better." That which was with the Father, that fountain from which flows all wisdom and beauty and truth and immortality—for the sake of that, Paul gives it all up.

Paul knew that the human heart was idolatrous and would worship anything it possessed. Just about anything we get our hands on, we're likely to worship. As a little child takes his teddy bear to bed with him, we grown-ups have our teddy bears as well. We are too grown-up and mature to be caught taking a teddy bear to bed, but we have what must look to God like teddy bears and dolls, and we hang on to them. This is all right when you're a child, but even when they're grown, a lot of people still insist on hanging on to things. Whatever you hang on to, you worship because it gets between you and God, whether it be property, family, reputation, security, or your life. Jesus taught us that we could not even hang on to life itself. What if we made living here on earth something we would not give up and tried to hang on to it? It would get in our way, and we would lose ourselves in the end.

We are often grasping after security. Yet Paul was not secure, and he said he "died daily." He was out at sea for three weeks, night and day, and he was always in difficulty. "Brethren," he said, "I give it all up. I disavow and disown everything."

Now, there were certain things God let the apostle Paul have. He let him have a book or two, a garment, and a cloak. In one instance, He let him have his own hired house for two years. He let him have some things, but Paul never let them touch his heart. Any external treasure that touches our hearts is a curse. Paul said, "I give all this up that I might know Him, that I might go on to a deeply enriched and increasing intimacy and vast expanses of knowledge of the One who is illimitable in His beauty."

To Paul, Jesus Christ was so infinitely attractive that he did not count anything else as amounting to anything. He was a highly educated man who learned at the feet of Gamaliel. He earned what today we would call a PhD. Despite this, Paul said, "That's all dross." He used an ugly word that meant *garbage*. He said, "It's no good. I put it all behind me." Then he testified, "I'm of the tribe of Benjamin, and I'm circumcised the eighth day, and I belong to the fathers. I got the marks upon me, and my name is in the register, and I can show you who I am. But for the sake of Jesus Christ, I count that nothing at all. I count it but loss."

The author of *The Cloud of Unknowing* wrote, "But one thing I tell thee, he that is God, he's a jealous lover, and he suffers no rival." That defines many of us today: we have allowed rivals to come into our lives and hearts. The result is that God isn't in there by himself. He warns, "If I'm not in your heart by myself, I won't work." He will work only after His Son Jesus Christ has cleaned everything, the bad and the good, from the temple and dwells there alone.

Heavenly Father, I surrender all to Thee. I will not allow any thing or any person to come between me and Thee. My love for Thee will be eternally exclusive. Amen.

BRIGHTNESS OF THE
FATHER'S GLORY

Brightness of the Father's glory,
Shall Thy praise unuttered lie?
Fly, my tongue, such guilty silence,
Sing the Lord who came to die.

Did archangels sing Thy coming?
Did the shepherds learn their lays?
Shame would cover me ungrateful,
Should my tongue refuse to praise.

From the highest throne of glory,
To the cross of deepest woe—
All to ransom guilty captives;
Flow, my praise, for ever flow.

Go, return, immortal Saviour,
Leave Thy footstool, take Thy throne;
Thence return and reign for ever;
Be the Kingdom all Thine own.

Robert Robinson

8

THE COMPONENTS OF
CHRISTIAN MATURITY

Yea doubtless, and I count all things but loss for the excellency of the knowledge of Christ Jesus my Lord: for whom I have suffered the loss of all things, and do count them but dung, that I may win Christ.

Philippians 3:8

God's work reminds me of the miner toiling away underground. If you've ever been near a mine where workers are deep in the earth, down there extracting coal, gold, or diamonds, you know that anyone could fly, walk, or drive by the area without having any idea what is happening. They're completely unaware that valuable jewels are being removed covertly from that place by an intelligent force. I believe God does that very thing in the human heart; He works deep within us, hidden and unseen.

Many prefer the dramatic, however, and do not want God to work unless He comes with a beard and a staff, playing the part. We want Him to be theatrical and do the thing with a good deal of color and pyrotechnics. But God does not work like that. He says, "No, no, you children of Adam, you children of carnality and lust, I won't work in you who have been brought up wrong and have wrong ideas about my Son."

Jesus works quietly, and He works alone. He says, "I can't work in your will or your heart unless I can be there alone." What some need to do is cleanse their temple. Get busy and throw out everything. Drive out the cattle, upset the money changers, shovel out the dirt, and eliminate all things that rival the Lord Jesus Christ.

As I mentioned earlier, in *The Cloud of Unknowing*, the author offers these words: "He's a jealous lover, and he suffers no rival." Reading that for the first time caused me to evaluate my experience with God. What has been a rival in my life? And what have I done about it? The author goes on to explain. "Lift up thine heart now unto God, with a meek stirring of love; and mean himself, and none of his goods. And thereto, look the slough to think on ought but himself." The key to what he's saying here is that our focus can only be on God. To focus on anything other than God is to move away from our relationship with Him. Only He matters, and nothing must be allowed to come between. This has to be essential in our pursuit of Christian maturity, and yet many don't understand that.

There must be more of "himself" these days and less of "ourselves." Christianity has become a way of getting things from God. We give a tithe so that our nine-tenths will go further than our ten-tenths. A man who would do that is not spiritual but is just doing it as good business. That's not what the Bible teaches or what Paul was talking about. We mustn't give to God as a means of getting for ourselves.

If we are going to mature in our Christian experience, our purpose is to forget all the things that God made so that our thoughts and desires are instead centered on God himself. Following the Lord does not always mean financial prosperity. In fact, it rarely does. Historically, following the Lord has meant counting those things but loss for the excellency of the knowledge of Christ. When a mature person in Christ prospers despite himself, he finds himself giving everything away except enough to live on. He is thankful for having a place to live and a car to take him to church and to work. Further than that, though, is not of much concern.

The apostle Paul knew this when he said, "I count all things but loss for the excellency of the knowledge of Christ Jesus my Lord: for whom I have suffered the loss of all things, and do count them but dung, that I may win Christ." He is saying that we need to let material things be and take no heed to them or their value. This is why many do not grow spiritually. What Paul's life demonstrated was the cry of a hungry soul. "O God, we don't want anything you have; we want *you*." That is the cry of the Christian on their way to maturity.

Some Christians would prefer to have a deeper life that could be given to them with a glass of water and a pill, say, three times a day. Some seem to think that is how following the Lord works. They want it in pill form, and they even want to buy a book instructing them on how to take that pill. Yet there is no such thing. Instead, there's a cross, a gallows, a man with stripes on his back, an apostle with no property, and a tradition of loneliness, weariness, and rejection. No pills.

Let us stop trying to promote our business by using God to do it. Let us stop trying to promote anything using God to do it. Put everything away but God, for He does not work in our hearts unless He can be there alone. This is what it means to love the Lord with all our hearts, with all our souls, and with all our minds (Matthew 22:37). Prayer is not just getting on our knees; prayer is the elevation of the heart to God. That is all that's needed. You can pray anywhere you find yourself. You can pray anywhere and worship God because it is himself that we seek, himself that we want. Just Him. Before long you will be trembling with rapture in the presence of the Lord Jesus Christ.

Therefore, lift your heart to God, put away things and your desire for property, and seek Him alone. Let Him work in you without any rival. And do not let anybody hinder you in your seeking after God, but instead prevail there until you sense the desire for Him. You become something other than a carnal Christian when you seek a new height. The first thing you will find is the devil facing you to stop you. Do not stop because of that but press right on. There are two times to pray: when you feel like it and when you don't. Some want to be emotionally lifted and walk on the clouds, but the old saints knew better than that. They were practical men. They knew there were times when it was all about making a choice to seek Him through prayer.

What we need is an unmitigated intent to know God, to know Christ, to put the world and things beneath our feet, and to open our hearts to one lover only, and that is the

Son of God himself, and keep everything else out. All other relationships—spouses, parents, children, siblings, friends—all those we keep outside ourselves. Deep in our hearts we have but one lover, and He suffers no rival.

You may ask, "Why does God make it so hard?" We are told only what we can understand. That being said, you proceeded, maintained your faith, and prayed, both when you felt like it and when you didn't. You trusted Christ and believed in God. You made the necessary corrections and adjustments in your home, workplace, and relationships, and gave up on the bad habits. You gave up things that were impeding you. The cross enters your life if your intent is pure and sincere and directed toward God. That's the kind of Christian you will be—you'll just keep going. Even if you don't feel that way, you will still believe the truth and pray to God with a sincere intent.

God will bring forth a Bethel from your stormy grief. He will raise you up into the sky, and you will emerge from the tomb. Then He draws you up out of the darkness into the light. There are times when I sit down looking as if I were dead, but in my heart there is such a joy lifting me toward God that I could shout. Do you want what I'm talking about? Do you want to move past the low level of the carnal Christian and know Him and the power of His resurrection and the fellowship of His sufferings and the excellency of His knowledge, leading to increasing flights of spiritual elevation? I think you do or you would not be this far in the book.

But to win Christ Jesus is to have everything in my life that was in His life when He walked among us—the suffering Christ endured, the opposition He faced. To believe that being a Christian is an easy, comfortable life is not to know the truth of God's Word. Separating ourselves from the world around us is the price of Christian maturity, but this means we get to come into the adoring presence of God.

O Father, how my heart yearns for Thee and Thee alone. I no longer desire what I once desired, and You have satisfied that desire for me. Amen.

HIMSELF ALONE

Once it was the blessing,
Now it is the Lord;
Once it was the feeling,
Now it is His Word.
Once His gift I wanted,
Now the Giver own;
Once I sought for healing,
Now Himself alone.

Once 'twas painful trying,
Now 'tis perfect trust;
Once a half salvation,
Now the uttermost.
Once 'twas ceaseless holding,
Now He holds me fast;
Once 'twas constant drifting,
Now my anchor's cast.

Once 'twas busy planning,
Now 'tis trustful pray'r;
Once 'twas anxious caring,
Now He has the care.
Once 'twas what I wanted,

Now what Jesus says;
Once 'twas constant asking,
Now 'tis ceaseless praise.

Once it was my working,
His it hence shall be;
Once I tried to use Him,
Now He uses me.
Once the pow'r I wanted,
Now the Mighty One;
Once for self I labored,
Now for Him alone.

Once I hoped in Jesus,
Now I know He's mine;
Once my lamps were dying,
Now they brightly shine.
Once for death I waited,
Now His coming hail;
And my hopes are anchored,
Safe within the veil.

Albert B. Simpson

9

THE COMPLETENESS
OF CHRISTIAN MATURITY

Not that I speak in respect of want: for I have learned, in
whatsoever state I am, therewith to be content.

Philippians 4:11

As maturing Christians, we aim to know and win Christ—to
know the power of His resurrection, conform to His death,
and experience Christ in His fullness. To do that is to count
all things but loss for the excellence of His knowledge.

There is a prayer from the author of *The Cloud of Unknowing*, saying he wants God "to so help us that we may
have the intents of our heart so cleansed that we may perfectly love God and worthily praise Thee." I cannot repeat
that too many times. We seek a place in God where we may
perfectly love and praise Him, not only judicially but expe-
rientially in ourselves that which we have in Christ and be

united with Him here in this world. This is New Testament Christianity.

Our Christian maturity rests upon the work of the Holy Spirit in our lives and hearts. The Spirit's mission is (a) to persuade Christians that this is possible and (b) to lead them, as Joshua led Israel, into the Promised Land. Making these two a reality in the Christian's life is impossible for man, but not for the Spirit of God. For a persuaded mind and a well-intentioned heart are far from faithful practice, which seems to describe the carnal Christian. Although they believe the right things to a degree, they are not flourishing as mature Christians; rather, they remain mediocre. Jesus said, "Wherefore by their fruits ye shall know them. Not every one that saith unto me, Lord, Lord, shall enter into the kingdom of heaven; but he that doeth the will of my Father which is in heaven" (Matthew 7:20–21).

Perhaps for many of you readers, recent years have been your worst time spiritually. You hope to grow, but you have been more discouraged than ever before, filled with doubts and defeats. Instead of being encouraged by what you have been learning, you have found that it has cast you down. Those who have been so discouraged, who have known the rat teeth of doubt eating at them, and who have bumped their chins on the sidewalk due to defeats, they are the ones getting nearer to God.

Conversely, others can still be worldly and not mind it. But those who have found the way difficult, with things working against you as you long and yearn to know Jesus Christ, these are the ones who are very close to the kingdom.

I want to share another phrase from the book *The Cloud of Unknowing*, which sums up the Bible's teaching on this issue. The author states, "See who by grace may see," or to put it in the language of the Scriptures, "He that hath ears to hear, let him hear" (Matthew 11:15). God sifts out those who cannot hear so that He may lead on by grace those who can. Remember, though Israel "be as the sands by the seashore, yet a remnant shall be saved." The Lord said that, in the last days, few should be found in the right.

Gideon was going up against the enemy, and they had 32,000 soldiers (Judges 7). The Lord said, "You have too many; let them go who by grace may." He said anyone who is afraid should turn back, and 22,000 out of the 32,000 turned back. Then God said, "You still have too many. I can see people among you who cannot see and who you'll never be able to make Israelite soldiers out of. Test them." So Gideon led them to the river and tested them, and once it was all over, he had only 300 remaining.

Only the tested will be able to go forward into Christian maturity. If you want to know why you're struggling, why your efforts to grow with God have only gotten you into more difficulty, remember Christ's journey to immortal triumph. Remember the garden where He sweat great drops of blood? Remember Pilate's Hall where they put a purple robe on Him and beat Him? Remember the desertion when the disciples forsook Him and fled? Remember the journey up the hill to Calvary? Remember His being nailed to the cross? Remember the six hours, the hiding of the Father's face? Remember the darkness and the surrender of His Spirit in death? This was the path Jesus took to immortal triumph and everlasting glory, and as He is, so are we in this world.

Some may call this the dark night of the soul. Scarcely a Christian is willing to enter this dark night of the soul, which is why very few proceed into the light. They do not know the morning because they will not face the night. And the Holy Spirit cannot do His work if there is something in the way, something the Christian is holding back in their heart, not fully surrendered. If you find yourself seeking but still troubled, still kept from entering the Promised Land, it may be because you have yet to come to the end of yourself. Too often we interfere with God's work in us. Again, we need to let Him alone while staying in a place of humility and meekness.

Many Christians get in the habit of hiding their inner state, but the Bible teaches that we ought to expose our inner state, not hide it. And because we hide it, God cannot change it. When we hide, we disguise our poverty of spirit. We refuse to admit to ourselves and to God just how poor we are in spirit. Why do we disguise our poverty of spirit and hide our inward state? Is it to preserve our reputation and keep some authority to ourselves? Why do we avoid turning the last key over to Christ? We want to have dual control, letting the Lord run our lives while still keeping some control ourselves in case the Lord fails. That will not do. We must turn over *all* authority, for not doing so will prevent us from maturing as Christians.

In his book *The Inner Life*, François Fénelon wrote, "We are strangely ingenious in perpetually seeking our interest, and what worldly souls do crudely and openly, people who want to live for God often do more subtly." It is almost humorous, but it is so true that we are strangely ingenious in seeking our own interests under the guise of seeking the interest of God. With the help of some pretext that serves as a screen, people tend to reveal only their best selves to others, thus preventing them from glimpsing the ugliness inside. We want to keep some glory for ourselves. We are willing to pray, "And lead us not into temptation, but deliver us from evil: For thine is the kingdom, and the power, and the glory, for ever. Amen" (Matthew 6:13), but too often we still desire to keep a little of the glory for ourselves.

Some people use missions, healing, prophecy, the deeper life, and all the rest for no other purpose than to secretly promote their private interests. By using such things as a pretext and letting the pretext serve as a screen, they will never know how ugly they are inside.

Though nobody wants to die on a cross, Paul said he wanted to know what it was like to be crucified, so that if he died like Christ, he might have a superior resurrection. We may be willing to die a little bit at a time, but we always try to rescue some part of ourselves, and that part of yourself will keep you from entering the Promised Land. It is possible to want to be filled and yet resist the filling, to plead to be filled and at the same time hinder God from filling you. We beg Him to help us, and then like stubborn children we won't let Him do so. What worldly people do crudely, we who live for God often do more subtly. In the eyes of God, of course, it is not subtle at all. It is only subtle to us. Either way, this living in a state of contradiction acts as a hindrance to our growth as Christians.

A man on the cross is not happy. It is when he gets over that and cries, "Father, into thy hands I commend my spirit," and ceases to defend himself and let go, it is then that he dies. And there's a resurrection that follows. That, though, is what needs to happen if we are ever going to be anything more than carnal, mediocre Christians and move from where we are to where we ought to be.

If there is anything you are not willing to let go of and quit calling your own, you will never see this fullness of Christian maturity. The Lord has been saying to you, "Look to me and let go," but you've refused Him. What you refuse to relinquish to God takes up the space in your life that the Holy Spirit wants to fill. He can never fill it, however, and you will never know that fullness, until everything is completely turned over to the Lord.

A life of victory in Christ Jesus awaits us, a union with Him that will lift us above our troubles, guide us through the dark valley of dying and death, and lead us out into unbounded freedom and joy.

O God, I long for the fullness of Thyself in me. Whatever the cost, I'm willing to bear it. I step aside and give You complete control of my life for Your good pleasure and glory. Amen.

BRING YOUR VESSELS, NOT A FEW

Are you longing for the fullness of the blessing
of the Lord
In your heart and life today?
Claim the promise of your Father, come according
to His word,
In the blessed old time way.

He will fill your heart today to overflowing,
As the Lord commandeth you,

90

"Bring your vessels, not a few;"
He will fill your heart today to overflowing
With the Holy Ghost and pow'r.

Bring your empty earthen vessels, clean thro' Jesus'
    precious blood,
Come, ye needy, one and all;
And in human consecration wait before the throne of
    God,
'Till the Holy Ghost shall fall.

He will fill your heart today to overflowing,
As the Lord commandeth you,
"Bring your vessels, not a few;"
He will fill your heart today to overflowing
With the Holy Ghost and pow'r.

Like the cruse of oil unfailing is His grace for
    evermore,
And His love unchanging still;
And according to His promise with the Holy Ghost
    and pow'r,
He will ev'ry vessel fill.

He will fill your heart today to overflowing,
As the Lord commandeth you,
"Bring your vessels, not a few;"
He will fill your heart today to overflowing
With the Holy Ghost and pow'r.

Lelia N. Morris

10

THE WILL OF GOD IN CHRISTIAN MATURITY

Then said I, Lo, I come: in the volume of the book it is written of me, I delight to do thy will, O my God: yea, thy law is within my heart.

Psalm 40:7–8

Our relation to the will of God is both passive and active. It's passive in that it is a resignation to God's will. When we mention God's will today, we almost invariably mean, and are understood to mean, a resignation to God's will. We sing about God's will, and we understand what Mary meant when she said, "Be it unto me according to thy word" (Luke 1:38). That was something God was going to do, but not something Mary was going to do; that is resignation and passivity. It is necessary and good to say, "God, I accept your will for me."

Then there's the other relation to the will of God, which is rarely talked about: the active side of the will of God. Voluntary observance of God's commandments means changing your entire life as God indicates—to relinquish some things, take up others, and live one's life in accordance with the Word of God. I call this a reformation in the Church, which would result in a revival. If it cannot come to the whole Church, then I hope it comes to as many as will receive it, this active, voluntary observance of God's commandments.

In one of his sermons, Paul Rader said that God heard Elijah because Elijah heard God, and that God did according to the word of Elijah because Elijah had done according to the Word of God. You cannot separate these two things. If we desire for God to hear us, we must first hear God.

There is a lot of passivity in the Church today. We sing, "Have thine own way, Lord, have thine own way," but we often have no idea what God's will is; we are passively resigned. But that is only a part of accepting His will. The other part is to hear the voice of God and do what we are told, which means being active, bringing the entire life into accord with the New Testament and the teachings of Christ.

The will of God is the place of blessed, painful, fruitful trouble. Paul called it the "fellowship of his sufferings" (Philippians 3:10). One of the reasons we have so little post-cross power is that we refuse pre-cross trouble and do not let God's will concern us too much. We would prefer to be passive, not allowing the will of God to lead to anything uncomfortable.

Remember this: you will find Christ in clear manifestation in the fellowship of His sufferings. I say with an upraised hand that if there is anything in this world I want, it is to have a clear and continuous manifestation of that presence, that one in whose presence my soul takes delight. If we do not have it, that is because we don't relate the will of God with Jesus' cross.

The saints of the Old Testament were well acquainted with the idea of the cross even before Christ's time. Before His cross was raised on the bloodied hill, they were acquainted with it because of their obedience. There was Jacob who observed the direction that his cross came from. His cross came from his carnal self. He did not see it at first, but he came to understand. Then there was Daniel whose cross was the world. There was Job, and his cross was the devil. We have the world, the flesh, and the devil in Jacob, Daniel, and Job. The devil crucified Job, the world crucified Daniel, and Jacob was crucified on the tree of his own Jacobness and carnality.

As for Moses, his cross was Egypt, the oppressor of God's people. There were also the apostles whose crosses came from the religious authorities. There was Luther whose cross came from the church that made so much of wooden crosses, the Catholic Church. There was John Wesley whose cross came from the Protestant church. I could go on down the line and name the great souls who obeyed and followed the will of God to their different crosses, and although it was before Christ's time in some instances, they all died on their cross as certainly as Paul did, who said, "I'm crucified with Christ." By faith they looked forward, and their obedience to the will of God led them to a place of blessed, painful, and fruitful trouble.

In our own day we cannot walk up the hillside and die. When Jesus was on earth, following Him physically was not hard. Anybody could get out of work, say good-bye to his family, and say, "I'm going to follow Jesus." Multitudes did. They followed Him physically but did not understand Him spiritually. However, your cross is not to follow Jesus along a dusty pathway. It is not to climb the hill where two others are being crucified. Our cross will be the trouble we get into by our obedience to the will of God. That is our identification with Christ himself.

I want Christians to take this seriously and seek to be one with God in a way that the careless evangelical world seems to consider either fanaticism or an old-fashioned way of thinking that they are not even discussing. It begins with identification with the cross, but resurrection must follow.

Some preach death so much that they never allow anybody up out of it. They preach death, death, death. When I was young, I was wonderfully filled with the Holy Spirit and was getting along, and then I read a book about the cross. That book puts you on the cross in the first chapter, and as far as I can remember, you were still hanging on the cross in the last chapter. The result was gloom all the way through. The writer himself was not a gloomy preacher, but somehow he got gloom into his book, and I had an awful time shaking it off.

There was another preacher, A. B. Simpson, whose approach to the cross was so radiantly wonderful that he jarred and blessed his generation. There is a cross, yes, but beyond that cross there is resurrection, identification, and manifestation. Simpson highlighted the manifestation of the presence of God himself. I do not mean any physical manifestation except that it would result in that tenderest manifestation of tears of joy. I mean a presence made known to the human spirit, and God is willing to give that. In the Welsh revival, that happened so much that sometimes the preacher could not even preach. We do not see that today, and nobody seems to want it.

We must have reformation before we can hope for a genuine revival.

I heard a phrase once that stayed in my mind: "God is ingenious in making our crosses." He makes our crosses out of iron and lead, which are heavy in themselves. He also makes them of straw, which seems to weigh nothing yet is no less difficult to carry. And He makes crosses of gold and precious stones, which dazzle the spectators and excite the envy of the public but crucify no less than the other crosses that are more despised.

Some people are into money, and that's their cross made of gold and precious stones. It dazzles and excites, but it is a cross nevertheless. God makes them of all the things we like best and then turns them into bitterness. It often pleases God to join physical weakness to the servitude of the spirit. Nothing is more useful than these two crosses together. They crucify a man from head to foot. God takes pleasure in confounding human power, which is only human weakness disguised.

Whatever kind of power you believe you possess, in the end it will bother you and get you in trouble. Say you have intellectual power, you've a great mind—that is good, and I'm glad you have it. Yet it's your great mind that will likely vex you and invite trouble into your life, for it is just human weakness in disguise. Still, it's good to have it, and God has so ordered such things. Whatever your talents, there is your weakness disguised. In fact, everything we have is tied to human weakness. God makes what the world admires, ridiculous and frightful, and He treats without pity those He raises without measure. He joins these crosses and crucifies the man from head to foot.

That phrase, God will crucify without pity those whom He wants to raise without measure, is crucial in coming through the will of God to Christian maturity. Some have experienced more dryness than they've ever known before. God uses our dryness, impatience, and discouragement to bring to birth within us humility, showing us our true selves. He does all this so that we might see and adore Him. For us to adore Him, He must slay us; and for us to love Him, he must crucify us.

Do you want to be raised without measure? Do you want God to say to all the angels and all creatures that do His will, "There's no limit to where I will take this man. There's no measure, no ceiling in what he can have. I'll raise him without measure, for it is without pity that I crucify him"?

It is the maturing Christians who are completely separated from all their prejudices and carnal desires, who are willing to place themselves in the hands of God, to bear any cross—iron, straw, gold, or any God thing—and be the kind of examples God desires. God is all; we only have to see and adore Him. There will come a time when all you have will be God and the cross.

How agonizing for those ones who have never understood and have never been taught and have no evangelical message at all that would have them clutching to their breast a cross when they're dying. Clutch it and hold it tight, knowing there is something to take them over the river. This is that cross which comes to you from being in the will of God. God lets me fall on my face, break my nose, do some fool thing or otherwise injure my soul, and that is the cross, and the Lord nailed me there. All we have to do is see and adore Him in it all.

You will discover that obedience brings the cross to life quicker than anything else. Your true cross is what you take from the hand of God, looking to Him, letting Him work, thanking and adoring Him. You would not change it if you could. Then comes the glorious resurrection, and the lift and the blessing.

I have a little prayer book I've carried with me for years. In it, I write down prayers, and I have reflected upon them throughout my life. A long time ago I wrote, "O God, let me die right rather than live wrong, rather than become hardened into another Christian who lives a poor life down on a low level."

I would rather die right than live wrong. Have you known the place of blessed sweet trouble, heart-searching, and travail? You can never know the blessing and the glory if you haven't. You can pray for revival, but you will never receive it. You can join groups and pray all night for revival, and all you lose will be sleep.

If we believe in this kind of reformation, why don't we do something about it? Who will lay their glory in the dust as best as he knows how? Before the Lord, seek the will of God in obedience, the will of the cross in the identification and the presence and the glory and the resurrection and the life; who will do that?

O God, let me die right rather than live wrong, rather than become hardened down into another Christian who lives a poor life on a low level. Whatever the cost, I accept it in humble expectation of Thy glorious presence in my life. Amen.

ALL THE WAY MY SAVIOR LEADS ME

All the way my Savior leads me—
What have I to ask beside?
Can I doubt His tender mercy,
Who through life has been my guide?
Heav'nly peace, divinest comfort,
Here by faith in Him to dwell!
For I know, whate'er befall me,
Jesus doeth all things well;
For I know, whate'er befall me,
Jesus doeth all things well.

All the way my Savior leads me—
Cheers each winding path I tread,
Gives me grace for ev'ry trial,
Feeds me with the living bread.
Though my weary steps may falter
And my soul athirst may be,
Gushing from the rock before me,
Lo! a spring of joy I see;
Gushing from the rock before me,
Lo! A spring of joy I see.

All the way my Savior leads me—
Oh, the fullness of His love!
Perfect rest to me is promised
In my Father's house above.
When my spirit, clothed immortal,
Wings its flight to realms of day,
This my song through endless ages:
Jesus led me all the way;
This my song through endless ages:
Jesus led me all the way.

Fanny Crosby

11

THE HEART OF
CHRISTIAN MATURITY

My tears have been my meat day and night, while they continually say unto me, Where is thy God?

Psalm 42:3

My passion determines the pursuit of my Christian maturity.
As David's heart was stirred after God and would not allow
anything to come between him and God, so should our passion be today as we grow in Christ.

There is a vast difference in tone between today's Christians and Psalm 42. Think, for instance, about this man
David. Look at how he sought after the Lord throughout the
book of Psalms. The language of David is found throughout
the Old Testament, beginning with Abraham and tracing
down from there. The gap between them and us, between
the tone of their lives and ours, is that they sought Him

and found Him and sought Him still, and they sought Him again and sought Him more and more. Their seeking never stopped. We believe in Him, accept Him, and then we tend to seek Him no more.

Reading about these great shining souls is music to our hearts, but they are dead and gone. We don't pray to them, and they have no virtue to give us. They got their virtue and merit from the same source, the same fountain, as we get ours: Christ Jesus our Lord. Though we're not deifying or canonizing them, their names are music to our ears because they're associated with this thirst Paul expressed in the verse discussed earlier. "Yea doubtless, and I count all things but loss for the excellency of the knowledge of Christ Jesus my Lord: for whom I have suffered the loss of all things, and do count them but dung, that I may win Christ" (Philippians 3:8).

The apostle goes even further: "Brethren, I count not myself to have apprehended: but this one thing I do, forgetting those things which are behind, and reaching forth unto those things which are before" (Philippians 3:13). The important phrase here is "reaching forth." No matter where Paul was in his Christian experience, he reached for what God had before him.

Henry Suso, in his book *The Little Book of Eternal Wisdom*, wrote, "It is one thing to hear for oneself a sweet lute, sweetly played, and quite another thing merely to hear about it." This seems to be the attitude of many Christians. They only hear that there has been a lute playing, but they have never heard it played themselves.

Reflect on all those saints down through the years whose names are musical because we associate them with thirsty souls. We see them as the deer being chased by hounds, thirsting, longing for water, and saying, "Let me alone, for my soul is seeking God." They found Him, and they sought Him again and again, never ceasing.

What a tragedy that we have been taught to believe in Him, accept Him, and then seek Him no more. But that's missing the point; direction and motion matter. We must point our target at God continually. Once again I cite that old book, *The Cloud of Unknowing*, and its words "Evermore crying after him thou lovest." Is that the testimony of your soul? We can only mature in our Christian experience with this kind of passion. We can never have enough of God.

There is a book of the Old Testament called the Song of Solomon that few people have read because it is a little raw. Most people do not read it because they do not know what it means, but it was the very joy of these great souls. And there's a song by Joseph Swain, "O Thou, in Whose Presence," whose lyrics were taken directly from the Song of Solomon. Following is the first stanza:

> "O Thou, in whose presence my soul takes delight,
> on whom in affliction I call;
> my comfort by day, and my song in the night,
> my hope, my salvation, my all."

The Song of Solomon is a story of a girl deeply in love with a young shepherd. She is so beautiful that a king demanded her favors. She stayed loyal to her shepherd, her simple shepherd who gathers lilies in the dew of the night and comes to seek her and call on her through the lattice. It is a wonderful love story indeed. It has been understood so by the Church as Jesus the shepherd, the rejected shepherd, and the world, with all its offers, is the king demanding, coaxing, trying to woo and win our love. At the same time, the shepherd waits, gathering lilies at night, staying true.

This is the kind of passion we so desperately need. The Church never runs on its head; the Church runs on its heart. Remember that the Holy Spirit never fills a person's head; the Holy Spirit fills a person's heart. The author of *The Cloud of Unknowing* said, "Be wary in this work; travail not in thy wits nor in thy imagination." In your longing after God, do not try to think your way through, because you will find in all this an element of unknowing—the deep, divine abyss of the Godhead.

We must not settle for anything less than this divine abyss, the soundless, undaunted sea of Being that we call God. It is there beyond the power of thought or visualization. It is utterly futile to try to think your way through. That has been our difficulty in the day in which we live. The young man feels hungry in his heart and goes to see a teacher, and the teacher sits him down and begins thinking with him. Pretty soon he goes away saying, "Thank you, thank you, Doctor." He thinks he is all fixed up, but he hasn't received a thing. He has been taught in his head, but his heart still goes away hungry.

Do not throw the head away; you will need it, and so can a man fill his head with all the creatures on earth and their works and even the works of God. That's all right. Through grace, men can have the fullness of knowledge, but of God himself can no man think. Not that you cannot think about Him, but you cannot think around Him, think equal to Him, or think out to Him. He may well be loved but not thought of or analyzed. By love may He be begotten, and by love beheld, but never by thought.

Today we are satisfied with the works of God and the theology of God. But you'll never get there that way because thought only engages the intellectual element in the gospel. One of the attributes of deity is intellect, and there is surely an intellectual element in the gospel that we call theology or doctrine, and that is necessary and right. However, it is different from what we need and from what we seek. We need that which we can't get through our heads. As William Cowper's song says, "The Spirit breathes upon the Word / And brings the truth to sight."

When the Spirit breathes on the Scriptures, they are much more wonderful than when they are merely taught or expounded. The expounding of the Word of God without the Spirit breathing on it can be, if not harmful, at least a useless thing. We sing the hymn "Break Thou the Bread of Life" by Mary A. Lathbury, with its words "Beyond the sacred page I seek you, Lord; / my spirit waits for you, O living Word." The hymn says "beyond the sacred page"—not apart from the sacred page, not away from the sacred page, not contrary to the sacred page, but *beyond* the sacred page I seek you, Lord.

The sacred page is not to be a barrier to block our way to God. The sacred page is not to be a substitute for God; millions make it that. The sacred page is not to be the end, but only the means toward the end, and God is the end. It is God himself we seek with a sincere intent.

The common error is that if we have the text, we have the experience, and most Christians settle for that. In truth, if we have the text, we have the text; the experience ought to result from the text, but you can have the text and not have the experience.

Years ago, I heard an appropriate illustration for today's Christians. There was a wealthy man who died and left a will. In that will he passed on to his only son all of his riches, which ran into the millions of dollars. The son got the will and carried it around, but he was hungry, destitute, wearing ragged clothes and wandering the streets. Someone stopped him and said, "Why, you poor fellow, you're in bad shape. You're ragged, your skin shows through, and you look hungry and pale."

"Oh," he answered, "don't talk that way to me. Listen to this." And he opened his will and read, "'And unto my dear son, Charles, I bequeath my bonds, stocks, property, and yacht.'" Charles was satisfied with the will but had never had it probated. He didn't get any of the things that were bequeathed to him; he simply had the will.

Knowing the will of God is one thing, but having the will of God is another. Let me demonstrate this through the progress of the high priest into the holy of holies as described in the Old Testament. The Temple consisted of three places. The first was the outer court, which had no roof over it, and the sun shone down onto it. When the priest was there, he had the light of nature. Then he passed through a veil, and when the veil fell back in place, it was called the holy place. There was no light of nature, only an artificial light that the priests themselves made lit, but that was not enough.

Then there was the holy of holies, where a kind of glory burned and burned and burned, and there was no light of nature. The old intellect could not get in there, and there was no artificial light, no ecclesiastical light, no preacher intoning in a ministerial drawl. None of these could help them there.

The supernatural light of God was sought in the holy of holies, and it shone from the mercy seat. When the priest showed up, he had absolutely nothing. Can you imagine being one of the high priests in those days, knowing that the infinite God who made heaven and earth was dwelling in fire between the cherubim's wings? The priest moved toward that God.

So there was a natural light above to help in the outer court, and that was very good. That is your denomination. Then the priest went a little farther and got an artificial light. That is your theology. But he had to go on until there was no natural or artificial light, but a supernatural shining. In the presence of the supernatural shining, the priest had nothing to protect him but the blood, and nothing to assure him but the character of God, and he was all alone.

Nobody could go into the holy of holies with the priest. They could help him, and his helpers would assist the priest with the veils, but they had to back away with their eyes averted. They could not enter into the holy of holies. That was for the priest and the blood, no one else. The blood protected him from the burning, for he would have burned up as a leaf in the fire, except the blood was there to protect him. He had no insurance, nobody there to pat his back, nobody to show him a text, nobody to read to him, nobody to tell him a story, nobody to help him through it. He had nothing but the character of God to assure him, and he was all alone.

When you finally meet God, it has to be alone in your heart. You have yet to be converted if it takes a crowd to convert you. If it takes a crowd to get you through to the fullness of the Holy Spirit, you have not had and do not know anything about what I am saying here. There is aloneness there.

Most people do not want to be alone with God. Instead, they want a crowd around them, other people who are full of laughter, there to take the heat off. We want friends around us who can support us and comfort us. But if you ever get through to where you should be, and if your longing heart finds water, it will be while alone. I don't mean there will not be others with you, but you will be alone nonetheless, even though a crowd may surround you.

My heart, O God, yearns for You and Your presence. What must I do to enter into Thy holy presence and worship Thee? I long for nothing less than Your presence. Amen.

DOWN IN THE VALLEY

Down in the valley 'midst lilies sweet scented,
There is the friend whom I love and revere.
Oh, I will follow His steps so contented
As on the breeze His sweet name I can hear.

O Thou, God's precious Son,
Who gave Thy life for me,
I am so thankful, Lord, that Thou loved me.

Thee I am seeking, oh, heed my imploring;
Whither in fragrance dost Thou take repose?

Where Thou at midday Thy flock art restoring,
Shaded from heat where the clear fountain flows?

O Thou, God's precious Son,
Who gave Thy life for me,
I am so thankful, Lord, that Thou loved me.

Now I have found Thee, O Jesus, my Savior;
Let me eternally say, Thou art mine.
Hide not Thy face from the soul seeking favor;
Hast Thou not sought me and said I am Thine?

O Thou, God's precious Son,
Who gave Thy life for me,
I am so thankful, Lord, that Thou loved me.

Sweet as Thy voice have the angels ne'er spoken;
Soft as Thy smile can the light never be.
Press me so near to Thy heart in love's token.
Oh to be Thine, that means heaven to me.

O Thou, God's precious Son,
Who gave Thy life for me,
I am so thankful, Lord, that Thou loved me.

S. C. Ramsey

12

THE FOCUS OF
CHRISTIAN MATURITY

I will rise now, and go about the city in the streets, and in the
broad ways I will seek him whom my soul loveth: I sought
him, but I found him not. The watchmen that go about the
city found me: to whom I said, Saw ye him whom my soul
loveth?

Song of Solomon 3:2–3

To fully understand this pursuit of our Christian maturity,
we must understand that God deals with each of us as if we
were the only person in the universe. God must cut every
maverick out of the herd and brand that person alone. He
does not do it by group, but one by one. The three thousand
souls who were converted in the book of Acts were all converted each one alone as if there had been no others. When
the Holy Spirit came at Pentecost and rested upon those

who were there, the Bible does not say the tongues of fire visited them en masse. It says, "There appeared unto them cloven tongues like as of fire, and it sat upon each of them" (Acts 2:3). Each one went through this experience as if he had been all alone.

I remember a person by the name of Holy Ann, a remarkable Irishwoman in Canada who is now with the Lord in heaven. Her reputation was that she could get God to do anything she asked Him to do. Those who knew her said, "Ann prays as if God were her father and He had no other children." That is exactly what I mean; that is our relationship with God in spiritual maturity.

We want to help each other, and that is good, but God wants each of us to press through alone where there is no natural light to help us. We cannot lean on anything natural. Denominations have their place, and I am not against them, but they can become a curse if we do not watch them. We lean too much on our denominations. I read a letter from a man in an evangelical magazine, who wrote, "I have accepted the doctrines of such and such denomination, and I expect to stay with them, so don't bother me." The sad thing about this letter was that he allowed somebody else to decide for him. Millions of people are content with their religious denomination because someone does their thinking for them. Somebody assures them. Somebody says a word of consolation. All the thinking has already been done, all the responsibilities taken up by someone higher up, and all they have to do is obey.

This is why certain denominations can hold their people. They never tell you it's about you and God alone. You have to find God as "the hart finds the water brook." You have to seek God by yourself. Yes, I'll help you and quote Scripture, sing to you, and do my best, but when God meets you, it will be by yourself. You cannot look to the authority of others. Nobody can say, "All right, it's done. As of today, this hour, I declare you all right." I almost thought that myself in earlier days. A happy woman once said to me, "I think you've got it," meaning I'd gotten to where I needed to be with God. I thank Him I found out better.

What we want today in the Church is for everyone to cry after God. The question is, What shall we do? What does it look like to cry after God? What does it look like to focus on Him?

There are no vacuums in the kingdom of God. A vacuum is an empty place with nothing, not even air. Nature abhors vacuums, and wherever there is a vacuum, unless it has a hard shell to protect it, air or water quickly rushes in and fills the empty space. The kingdom of God also abhors a vacuum. When you empty yourself, the Almighty God rushes in. The reason we are where we are is that we are satisfied with what we have. But if you have emptied yourself, you will find that God will come into that vacuum.

We are drawn from earth to things above, drawn out of ourselves. That is the trouble with so many of us. We have never been drawn to the things above, out of ourselves. What a happy hour when we have created that vacuum, and into that vacuum rushes God's blessed presence. And by completely resigning to His perfect will and submitting ourselves to Him, we subject ourselves not only to Him but also, because of our love of Him, to every other creature. All of this should be willed and done by us simply for the glory of God, for His pleasure alone and because He wills and merits to be loved and served. This is the law of God impressed by the hand of the Lord himself in the hearts of His faithful servants. "For my yoke is easy, and my burden is light" (Matthew 11:30).

Whenever the Holy Spirit speaks, He says the same thing to everybody. I have mentioned the names of great characters in the Bible, from David on down. You can read their hymns and devotional books, and you will find that they all add up to the same thing, because the Holy Spirit does not say multiple things. No, He says the same thing to everybody who is listening. I can quote from anywhere in Scripture or from nearly any of the great hymns without fear of contradiction because the same Holy Spirit says the same thing to all of God's children. He says, "Pour yourself out. Give yourself up to me; empty yourself."

> "Bring your empty earthen vessels,
> clean through Jesus' precious blood,
> Come, ye needy, one and all;
> And in human consecration
> wait before the throne of God,
> Till the Holy Ghost shall fall."
>
> Lelia N. Morris

Study the hymns, and you will find they all say the same thing: wait for the glory of God alone, for God himself, not mentally, not intellectually, but through the Holy Spirit. "For what man knoweth the things of a man, save the spirit of man which is in him? even so the things of God knoweth no man, but the Spirit of God" (1 Corinthians 2:11). Who knows of the things of God, but the Holy Spirit, who will help you to climb your way up Jacob's ladder, head over heels into the kingdom. You cannot think your way through; you can only love your way in and believe your way in. Come in meekness like a child and be drawn by your Redeemer's love. Come and pour yourself out until, at last, you are delivered from yourself. That is your only problem: yourself. You say, "I'd be a better Christian if I had a better pastor." I wish that could be so, but you know it would not be. The better the pastor, the more peril you would be in because of the tendency to become a spiritual parasite and lean on your pastor instead of the Holy Spirit.

Often the most spiritually mature people can be found in churches where the pastor cannot preach his way out of a wet paper sack. The reason is that, having received little help from the pulpit, they are seeking God alone. But if you get too much help from the pulpit, you're at risk of becoming a spiritual parasite by leaning on the pastor. I do not want anybody to lean on me, because I believe in the priesthood of the believer. There are those in the pews who surely hear God's voice and have as much right to speak as I have. I like the way Charles Spurgeon put it: "No man ever laid his empty hands on my empty head." He was speaking of ordination, meaning that if the Almighty God has not called the man, you can ordain him until the cows come home and he will still be lifeless.

You are your trouble. It's just you; if you get delivered from yourself, you will be drawn out at last. And what a noise it will make when you are drawn out of yourself! You are stuck so far down in the mud of your ego that when God pulls you out, a sound will be heard a block away. Stop thinking you are somebody, and stop thinking you are a theologian. God can be loved, and by love He may be gotten. He may be held by love but never by thought. Seek God in your own heart.

I do not mean it is wrong to go to altars and prayer rooms to pray; I'm talking about the loneliness of the soul that may be cut out of the crowd, cut out all by itself, like the woman who pushed her way through to Jesus. Jesus was so crushed in the crowd that they pressed him on every side. But one lonely little woman pushed through and touched His cloak and was healed. "And Jesus said, Who touched me? When all denied, Peter and they that were with him said, Master, the multitude throng thee and press thee, and sayest thou, Who touched me?" (Luke 8:45).

We can have crowds and meetings where people jostle along, but they are just jostling. Somewhere, though, some little soul pushes through and touches Him. She touched Jesus in love and faith, and the heart was healed. We, too, need to have our hearts healed and ointment put on them. "Is there no balm in Gilead; is there no physician there?" (Jeremiah 8:22). Yes, there is a balm in Gilead to heal the sin-sick soul.

Let me remind you that your beloved is gathering lilies like in the Song of Solomon. If you watch, you will see him put his hand through the lattice and say, "My beloved spake, and said unto me, Rise up, my love, my fair one, and come away" (Song of Solomon 2:10). At first the poor bride didn't respond. She said, "Oh, I've got ointment on my hands, and my night garments on. I am on my couch. I could not possibly get out." Sadly, he went away. Then her heart began to condemn her. She jumped up, threw on a robe, and started after him. But then she said, "I could not find him. Oh, you daughters of Zion, have you seen the star that on Israel shone?"

He had tapped on the lattice, and she said, "I can't come now; I'm sorry, honey, I'm all covered with ointment." So he went sadly away to his work among the lilies. But she followed him. She went to the virgins and asked, "Have you found him?" They replied, "What is he above others that you are looking for him?" She said, "He is altogether lovely, and I was such a fool to miss it. He called and said come on, come on, come springtime. I heard him but did not have the heart to go, but now I see what I missed."

At last she found him, and when she found the one she loved, she said, "Who is this coming forth pure as the sun, bright as the sun, and clear as the moon, terrible as an army with banners?"

My friend, He is very near to us and always will be. He is near, and He waits. He waits for a vacuum to form inside your heart. You may ask, "What is in my heart?" I do not know, but whatever it is, you need to get it out. And when you pour it out, He will rush in.

My heart seeks for Thee, my Beloved. I long to love you as you deserve to be loved. I will never stop seeking until I see Thee face-to-face in glory. Amen.

JUST A CLOSER WALK WITH THEE

I am weak but Thou art strong;
Jesus, keep me from all wrong;
I'll be satisfied as long
As I walk, let me walk close to Thee.

Just a closer walk with Thee,
Grant it, Jesus, is my plea,
Daily walking close to Thee,
Let it be, dear Lord, let it be.

Thro; this world of toil and snares,
If I falter, Lord, who cares?
Who with me my burden shares?
None but Thee, dear Lord, none but Thee.

Just a closer walk with Thee,
Grant it, Jesus, is my plea,
Daily walking close to Thee,
Let it be, dear Lord, let it be.

When my feeble life is o'er,
Time for me will be no more;
Guide me gently, safely o'er
To Thy kingdom shore, to Thy shore.

Just a closer walk with Thee,
Grant it, Jesus, is my plea,
Daily walking close to Thee,
Let it be, dear Lord, let it be.

Anonymous

13

THE THREATS TO CHRISTIAN MATURITY

For as by one man's disobedience many were made sinners, so by the obedience of one shall many be made righteous. Moreover the law entered, that the offence might abound. But where sin abounded, grace did much more abound: That as sin hath reigned unto death, even so might grace reign through righteousness unto eternal life by Jesus Christ our Lord.

Romans 5:19–21

About a generation ago, textualism captured the gospel or fundamentalist church—that is, those who believe in Christ the Savior and accept Him as such. The scribes and the lawyers took over and set up a hierarchy in schools, Bible conferences, and churches, and they all bought into it. The result was a rigid adherence to words.

I have never believed anything else but in the plenary, which means the full, verbal inspiration of the Scriptures as originally given. As a responsible Christian teacher, I believe every word of it. But the problem with the way this has been taught is that a rigor mortis sets in. The result was that religious imagination became stultified, religious learning choked off, religious aspirations slapped around, and the aspiring wings of the children of God were clipped like a hen in a hencoop. We were admonished to be quiet, accept what we were told, and that was it.

As this way of teaching the New Testament set in, you know what happened? There came about a revolt against these scribes in two directions. First, the Evangelicals revolted without realizing they were revolting. It was like the gasping of a fish in a bowl with no water or oxygen. The masses revolted into religious entertainment until the gospel churches are now camping on the doorsteps of the theater. Then, over against that and on the opposite side, some of the more astute fundamentalists and Evangelicals revolted into rationalism, which is already making peace with liberalism.

The result of all of this is that we rarely hear about Christian maturity anymore. On one side we have people saying, "I've accepted Jesus, whoop-de-doo, let's go have fun." And on the other side, serious, reverent believers are thinking their way near the borders of liberalism. Meanwhile, the New Testament objectives and methods have been allowed to lie dormant. In the name of the lordship of Jesus—which is lordship in name only—we have devised methods for achieving our objectives, which are, in many cases, not scriptural at all. I ask you: Is it a heresy to yield, pray, and long after God? Do such things constitute a radical mind?

You may remember the prayer in *The Cloud of Unknowing*, "God, I beseech thee so for to cleanse the intent of mine heart with the unspeakable gift of thy grace, that I may perfectly love thee, and worthily praise thee." To perfectly love God and worthily praise Him, even if it costs you everything, is that heresy? Should someone be ostracized for it? Considering our hymnody and devotional literature, which date all the way back to the apostle Paul, as well as the saints' biographies, the answer to that question is no.

Nicephorus's spiritual writings in the *Philokalia* start out by seeking to help Christians come to know God and do what *The Cloud of Unknowing* called being one with God, united with God. We Christians must ask ourselves, "Could I go along with this?"

Yet our wings have been clipped, the oxygen has been cut off, and our longings have become numb. Nicephorus was an eighth-century Greek Orthodox Christian. He was not a Protestant, and he was not a Roman Catholic; he wasn't a Coptic or a Nestor. He belonged on the Greek side, but he was a saint all the same. He wrote a little book, *On Watchfulness and the Guarding of the Heart*, to help people mature in God. In it he wrote, "You who desire to capture the wondrous divine illumination of our Savior Jesus Christ. Do you believe in this, who seek to feel the divine fire in your heart?"

He dared to use these words, writing to those who wished to feel the divine fire in their hearts, who strived to sense and experience reconciliation with God, to unearth the treasure buried in the field and to gain possession of it, having renounced everything worldly. Throughout Church history there have always been those who want to know and to receive the kingdom of heaven existing within them. While this is not a new doctrine, when many hear it, it sounds strange and different to them and they ask what it means.

Lady Julian of Norwich, in *Revelations of Divine Love*, said, "Our Lord God willeth we have great regard to all the deeds that He hath done: in the great nobleness of the making of all things; and the excellency of man's making, which is above all his works; and the precious Amends that He hath made for man's sin, turning all our blame into endless worship. In which Shewing also our Lord saith: 'Behold and see! For by the same Might, Wisdom, and Goodness that I have done all this, by the same Might, Wisdom, and Goodness I shall make well all that is not well; and thou shalt see it.' And in this He willeth that we keep us in the Faith and truth of Holy Church, not desiring to see into His secret things now, save as it belongeth to us in this life."

Could it be said sweeter than that?

Always remember that God's face is turned toward us. Do not allow the devil to convince you otherwise, and do not let doubt set in. Do not let anything or anyone tear you away from the glorious knowledge that the face of God is turned toward you. And if as a Christian the smiling face of God is turned toward you, why then do we not enjoy it? Why do we as Christians not capture the wondrous divine illumination of the Savior Jesus Christ? Why do we not feel the divine fire in our hearts? Why do we not strive to sense and experience our reconciliation with God and the knowledge of it? Why do we not gain possession of it?

Some may dismiss this by saying that a person's position is their possession, meaning that salvation alone is all anyone needs. But why is it that the candles of our souls do not burn more brightly even now? Why do we not have the conscious experience and not receive the kingdom existing within us? It is because there's a cloud of concealment between us and God's smiling face.

There has never been a day when the sun did not shine. The sun shines somewhere on earth every day, for there has never been a time since our God said, "Let the sun rule the day," that the sun has not shown itself. Even so, there are dark days and misty days and cloudy days, and days where it gets so dark that the chickens go to roost as if it's nighttime. Yes, there are dark days, yet the sun still shines as brightly as June's brightest, clearest day. Why does it not shine on the earth? Because there is a cloud of concealment between the sun and the earth. The sun is all right. The sun is up there, grinning broadly and just as bright, just as hot, and just as radiant as ever. However, it does not get through to the earth because of the clouds.

What do I mean when I say that God's face is turned toward us? Very simply, God looks in our direction and sees everything about us. God knows what is happening in our lives even before it happens. It is hard for me to comprehend that God takes delight in me. I can think of a thousand reasons why God should not be delighted in me. And when I run out of reasons, the devil will help me to think up a thousand more. That is one thing we need to always remember—the devil hates it that God is smiling in our direction. The devil will do everything possible to hinder us from accepting this truth.

But when God looks at me as a believer now, He does not see me as I once was, wallowing in human depravity. And it does not matter the level of depravity because depravity is depravity. The devil wants me to look back and see how bad I was and then whisper in my ear, "How could God ever love someone like you?" Then he points out all my past depravities.

That is when I need to remember the motto from *The Cloud of Unknowing*: "Look now forward and let be backward." I believe that the devil hates this phrase. And if the enemy detests the phrase, I want to embrace it and live by its words for the rest of my life.

It can be hard to look forward and forget about the past. After all, we are only human and try to look at ourselves through God's eyes. This is why I love the hymn "What a Wonderful Savior" by E. A. Hoffman, which begins, "Christ has for sin atonement made / what a wonderful Savior! / We are redeemed! The price is paid! / What a wonderful Savior!"

The only reason we can look forward with confidence is because "Christ has for sin atonement made." How could a God, as presented in the Bible, put up with a wretch like me? God does not see me through my depravity, but rather He sees me through His atonement for me.

Throughout my spiritual walk, I have refused to allow people to congratulate me, pat me on the back, and tell me what a wonderful preacher I am. They do not know that I have heard my sermon recordings and know that I am not a good preacher. But it is not what I can or cannot do; it is what God has already done through Christ's atonement.

God faces in my direction because He desires to. He created me after "His image and likeness." Even though Adam and Eve sinned in the Garden of Eden, "Christ has for sin atonement made." Yes, I am the product of Adam and Eve, but more important, I am the product of Christ's atonement. That is how God sees me.

God does not see me as I see myself, nor does He see me as other people see me. God looks at me through the lens of His Son, Jesus Christ. In the Garden of Eden, before depravity entered the scene, God walked with Adam and Eve in the cool of the day. That was His great delight. And that's His delight today. Because we have been created in His image and likeness, He delights in walking with us and having fellowship with us.

Because of this, we must face many enemies. Many seem to think that when you become a Christian, the battle is over, and now all you have to do is smile and wait to be whisked off to heaven. But I want to tell you that the worst days of your life will be *after* you have accepted Jesus Christ as your Lord and Savior. For all the enemies of God are arrayed against you to destroy you.

Of course, the devil cannot take away our salvation, though he can take away the joy of walking with the Lord. He can take away our victory in Jesus. If we are going to overcome our enemies, we need to recognize God's face smiling in our direction. No matter what I go through, God is delighted in my life.

It is a different story if I am not obedient and rebel against God. But if I'm walking in obedience and in the power of the Holy Spirit, I will be the greatest delight to God, and He will look upon me as though I were the only human being in all the earth. As a believer, my life is a reflection of Christ Jesus, who lived in this world for the glory of the Father. Thus our lives are to be a vehicle of glory to God.

O Father God, while I may not know my enemies
and the threat to my relationship with Thee, I do
know I can trust You in any situation. I take pleasure
in Thy grace. Amen.

HAVE THINE
OWN WAY, LORD

Have thine own way, Lord!
Have thine own way!
Thou art the potter,
I am the clay.
Mold me and make me
after thy will,
while I am waiting,
yielded and still.

Have thine own way, Lord!
Have thine own way!
Search me and try me,
Savior today!
Wash me just now, Lord,
wash me just now,
as in thy presence
humbly I bow.

Have thine own way, Lord!
Have thine own way!
Wounded and weary,
help me I pray!
Power, all power,
surely is thine!
Touch me and heal me,
Savior divine!

Have thine own way, Lord!
Have thine own way!
Hold o'er my being
absolute sway.
Fill with thy Spirit
till all shall see
Christ only, always,
living in me!

Adelaide A. Pollard

14

THE CLOUDS HINDERING CHRISTIAN MATURITY

The LORD make his face shine upon thee, and be gracious unto thee: The LORD lift up his countenance upon thee, and give thee peace.

Numbers 6:25–26

We know how clouds can conceal the sun from shining on us, but how does our Christian maturity become concealed? Clouds of concealment are the greatest challenges we will face in this journey of growing spiritually.

These are clouds we allow to hover over us as Christians, separating us from where we should be in Christ. Atonement has been made. There is nothing to do, for it has all been done. Not a drop of blood needs to be shed; not a spear needs to enter a holy heart, not a tear nor groan nor drop of sweat nor a moment in agony. Death has no more dominion over us; it is finished forever. The face of God shines down upon us. But even for Christians, there are clouds of concealment between "thee and thy God." Recognizing these clouds is a challenge, and only when a cloud is located can it then be addressed.

The first is the **Cloud of Pride.** You are your Father's child, and heaven is your home. Yet for a lifetime you may go without the wondrous, divine illumination of the Savior Jesus Christ, without feeling the divine fire in your heart, or sensing and experiencing that reconciliation with God—without the candle of your soul burning brightly because you have allowed the cloud of pride to remain over your head.

The devil says, "God hates you. God has turned His back on you." The devil lies constantly, but sometimes we believe his lies. The back of God has never been turned on a child of God nor a repentant sinner since the hour Jesus hung on the cross and said it was finished before death came. The face of God is turned our way, but we allow the cloud of pride to come between us and Him.

Another cloud that gets in our way is the **Cloud of Stubbornness.** Some people are just plain stubborn. They will not bend; they will yield neither to men nor God, nor to anybody except the law and death itself. Regarding this cloud of stubbornness, God complained about Israel: "Because I knew that thou art obstinate, and thy neck is an iron sinew, and thy brow brass" (Isaiah 48:4). God could not get Israel to yield because of their stubbornness. Our own stubbornness comes between God and us and keeps us from having what God wants us to have.

Then there is the **Cloud of Ambition.** Some Christians are religiously ambitious for something that is not in the will of God or that is for self-aggrandizement, resulting in a cloud between them and their God. There is a verse in Proverbs that is a perfect picture of the human heart. It says, "The foolishness of man perverteth his way: and his heart fretteth against the LORD" (Proverbs 19:3). Such people get tripped up by their own foolish ambition, finding fault even with God.

Instead, we must give up everything and be willing to follow wherever God leads us. Some try to pray through this cloud, but they cannot; nothing can penetrate it. They try to fast through it, but the cloud will not be lifted. If you think anything is yours, and you will not give it up, that will put a cloud over you. If there is any sun, it will not be very bright. Some think that if you pray long enough, everything will be all right, but God got Samuel up off his knees and told him to quit. "And the LORD said unto Samuel, How long wilt thou mourn for Saul, seeing I have rejected him from reigning over Israel? fill thine horn with oil, and go, I will send thee to Jesse the Bethlehemite: for I have provided me a king among his sons" (1 Samuel 16:1).

There are many illustrations throughout the Bible and in Church history where God stops people from praying. There is a time to pray, and then there is a time to get up and act on that prayer. Our modern idea is that everything will be okay if you pray long enough. But that's not true. The saint of God loves long seasons of prayer, and God answers prayer. Prayer is the soul's sincere desire, the breath of the soul, and I believe and practice all of that in some measure. But the idea that I can hang on to something and then pray the cloud away while clinging to the cloud is a terrible lie.

Another would be the **Cloud of Self-Love**. Even the Christian who has offered himself to Christ, believed in his conversion, that Christian can still keep a cloud of concealment over him simply by loving himself. To fall out of love with yourself is an injury, but a good one. It is like falling from a great height.

Then we have the **Clouds of Self-Gratulation and Self-Admiration**. The scribes in Jesus' day excused these, but we must come into a warm, personal, present, lasting fellowship with Jesus Christ that lifts us when we eradicate our hearts. Yet we cannot because we are proud of who we are, congratulate ourselves, and will not let anyone bother us.

Another challenge to our Christian maturity is the **Cloud of Money**. Money often gets between us and our God. Years ago, an evangelist I heard pointed out that you can take two dimes and shut out an entire landscape. You can take two dimes with you to the Great Smoky Mountains and shut out all the glorious, green rolling hills with them. Just place them in front of your eyes—that's all it takes. The mountains are still there, majestic in the shining sun, but you do not see anything because of the money in front of your eyes. It does not take much money either. We who do not have much money tend to make snide remarks about the rich man. You can have only ten dollars, but if it comes between you and your God, that cloud will conceal God from you.

The Lord tells us that we should not be afraid of man. However, some Christians walk around with the **Cloud of Fear** above them and are constantly afraid. They want to fit into society, and we are told this is what we must do. The schools are busy teaching children to adjust and to get along well, but if you have that as your ultimate goal, you will have a cloud of fear over your heart. The same is true when it comes to our friends and our loved ones, which is perhaps the hardest to relinquish, as well as the positions we hold, whatever they may be.

God is searching for those who will put behind them the **Cloud of Forgetting**. Put this cloud behind you to separate yourself from what used to control you. Paul said, "Forgetting those things which are behind, and reaching forth unto those things which are before, I press toward the mark for the prize of the high calling of God in Christ Jesus" (Philippians 3:13–14). God does not want anyone or anything to take His place in our hearts; He wants us to seek Him and Him alone.

The things behind Paul were a cloud, and if they had been in front of him, they would have shut out God. But Paul put behind him his defeats, mistakes, blunders, errors, wrongs, the times he fell on his face, and the time the Lord had to rebuke him for his pride. He put all this behind him and under his feet as a cloud of forgetting. We must do the same and not have any clouds "between thee and thy God."

That is the job of the mature Christian, to put the cloud of forgetting behind them. Some understand and will do this, while others have come up to Kadesh-barnea once a week for years, then turned back to the wilderness and wondered why sand is in their shoes. Enter the Promised Land and do not go back.

The face of God is smiling still, and He's stronger than any clouds the devil can blow between you and His face. God is waiting within the veil, waiting for you to move toward Him.

I remember boarding a plane at LaGuardia Field in New York a few years ago. It was around three o'clock in the afternoon, and the smiling, relaxed, friendly pilot came out and made a little speech. He knew some passengers might be worried because it was raining miserably that day. He said, "We are leaving in a moment, and the situation is this, friends. In fifteen minutes, we'll be in the sunlight." The weather report showed it would be clear from New York to Chicago. Though we entered the plane almost feeling our way through the fog and the mist, in fifteen minutes, just as the pilot said, we put the clouds under us and saw the bright shining sun above. As we flew higher, even the clouds became white beneath us. You who have flown a lot have had the experience of seeing great billows of whipped cream underneath you, white as an egg, and when you were underneath them and looked up, they were a misty, miserable thing that shut out the sun. Then, in a matter of minutes, you put them under you. It is a great feeling to take off in the fog and rain and then fly up into the sunshine.

Many people will never move up in their Christian maturity. It seems they would rather stay right down there in the fog and rain while the sun shines brightly above. They think the sun is not shining when it is. Put it under you, whatever it is, the cloud that is between you and your God.

Thy face, O God, is what I long for. I know that You are looking at me with delight. That delight was established when Thy Son died on the cross and rose on the third day. I surrender to Thee and cherish that smiling face shining down on me. Amen.

FACE TO FACE
WITH CHRIST MY SAVIOR

Face to face with Christ, my Savior,
Face to face, what will it be
When with rapture I behold him,
Jesus Christ who died for me?

Face to face I shall behold him,
Far beyond the starry sky;
Face to face in all his glory,
I shall see him by and by.

Only faintly now I see him
With the darkened veil between,
But a blessed day is coming
When his glory shall be seen.

Face to face I shall behold him,
Far beyond the starry sky;
Face to face in all his glory,
I shall see him by and by.

What rejoicing in his presence,
When are banished grief and pain;
When the crooked ways are straightened
And the dark things shall be plain.

Face to face I shall behold him,
Far beyond the starry sky;
Face to face in all his glory,
I shall see him by and by.

Face to face, oh, blissful moment!
Face to face, to see and know;
Face to face with my Redeemer,
Jesus Christ who loves me so.

Face to face I shall behold him,
Far beyond the starry sky;
Face to face in all his glory,
I shall see him by and by.

Carrie Ellis Breck

15

THE SELF-TRUST DANGER TO CHRISTIAN MATURITY

For I am the least of the apostles, that am not meet to be called an apostle, because I persecuted the church of God. But by the grace of God I am what I am: and his grace which was bestowed upon me was not in vain; but I laboured more abundantly than they all: yet not I, but the grace of God which was with me.

1 Corinthians 15:9–10

It would take a lot of effort to find anyone more confident in his Christianity than the apostle Paul. This man knew what he believed and knew where he stood with God. He knew God and was confident with a great cosmic confidence. Yet he was also the most self-distrustful.

For some readers it is difficult to understand what the apostle Paul was talking about in the passage above, but it all comes down to one thing essentially: Paul's personal triumph resulted from an entire and radical distrust of himself. Self-trust is the last great obstacle to spiritual triumph.

Paul was careful not to trust himself. Before man he was as bold as a lion, but before God, Paul could not say much, as he had no confidence in himself. In fact, his confidence in God was because of his lack of confidence in himself. As far as he trusted himself, he did not trust God. As far as he distrusted himself, he leaned upon God. Self-trust, respectability, and self-assurance come from what you hear about yourself, what your friends tell you about yourself, and what you think of yourself. This is the last great obstacle to Christian maturity. Just when we think we've gotten rid of all self-trust, we haven't.

More than four hundred years ago, Lorenzo Scupoli was one of those Protestants who during his lifetime was considered more or less a heretic because of his evangelical view that went against the views of the official churches of his day. In his book *The Spiritual Combat*, he wrote, "Distrust of yourself is so necessary to you in the spiritual combat that without it, you must hold it certain that you will not be able to obtain the desired victory." What I appreciate is the clear, sharp language Lorenzo employs here. He goes on to write, "We are much too easily inclined by our corrupt nature to a false opinion of ourselves. We presume vainly in our own strength."

This is a difficult flaw to comprehend, but it is most offensive to God, who loves us and desires from us a faithful recognition of every grace in us. He wants us to see that every grace and virtue proceeds from Him alone, for He is the fountain of all good, and nothing, not even a good thought, can come from us except that it be of His will.

A person can be converted, born again, walk around testifying for decades, and never find this out. We glibly quote Paul, but it never reaches us that this obstacle to spiritual victory is self-trust. After every sin that we know about has been put away in our seeking to serve God faithfully, and after all the self-sins we know about have been crucified, we think we have stopped boasting, stopped loving ourselves, and have put away all our sins. We reckon ourselves dead through Jesus Christ. But after we publicly humble ourselves by going to the altar, self-trust may be even stronger because it has more foundation to build on.

After putting away our sins, giving up our wealth, taking a lower position, and allowing ourselves to be shoved around with our noses rubbed in the dust, self-trust whispers its consolation. Many people take that consolation of self-whispering to be the Holy Spirit, which is why we are so weak when we think we are strong. Self-consolation and self-trust whisper, "Now you're far ahead of others. You've put sin behind you and have confessed and humbled yourself. With God's help you may trust yourself and expect victory to come and power to be at your side. You're not one of those dead ones. You're one of the alive ones."

Self tells us that we had to part with friends to push on. Self pats our backs, and we enjoy it. Self insists that we've humbled ourselves, so that now we may trust ourselves. We are on top; we're getting somewhere. Sure, we understand that we need God's help, but we can expect victory from now on. That's self-trust. Almost all the joy the average Christian feels is because of the back-patting they get from themself. And the deeper they go into the will of God, the more back-patting they indulge in.

Self whispers, "Certainly, you know better than others. You read Thomas à Kempis, and you're different; you love the old hymns, and none of that other junk is for you. You're a separated Christian; none of those movies are for you, none of the crazy modern stuff is for you. You are better."

You do not know what is happening because you are feeling good, and your feeling good is strictly you being comforted by a self that hasn't yet died. The self-trust is there after you think it is gone.

Why is self-trust wrong? Because it robs God to get its demands satisfied. In the book of Malachi, God said, "Ye have robbed me. But ye say, Wherein have we robbed thee?" (Malachi 3:8). The context here is tithing, but it applies to self-trust as well. We rob God when we take away from Him the acknowledgment that nothing good comes from ourselves. Anything good comes from God alone, as our brother Simon Goulart would say, who wrote, "God is a fountain of all good, and nothing, not even a good thought, can come from us except it comes from God. We take that away from God and give it to our converted and sanctified selves."

We should not dare to take away from God the ultimate, final trust in Him. Doing so misjudges God and man and holds God to be less than He is and man more than he is. This is the final trouble with us in our progress toward Christian maturity. We can go to school, study theology, learn how God is the source and fountain, and learn about His attributes in our hearts, but still believe God is less than He is and we are more than we are.

Suppose the moon could talk and had a personality. The moon might say, "I shine on the earth. Whenever I can reach the earth, I see the earth becomes beautiful." The mud would respond, "Listen, don't you know you're nothing by yourself? You don't shine at all; you reflect. It's the sun that shines."

The apostle Paul could boldly shine and talk about it because he knew he was not really shining. He knew he did not have a thing in himself that befitted heaven. It was the grace of God in him; it was God and not he. Thus Paul completely and radically distrusted himself.

No person ever really knows about themself. We do not know how weak we are, just as no person knows what they sound like. Everybody thinks they sound right until they hear their voice on tape. The most humbling thing happened to me when I had my first sermon recorded. After I heard it, I could never stand the sound of my voice because that recording did not lie. I have heard myself on tape dozens of times since, trying to work something out that I could use, but it always sounds terrible to me. But before I heard that first recording, I was told I had a fine preaching voice. Now that I've heard it, however, nobody can tell me that anymore.

No person knows how weak they are until God exposes them, and nobody wants to be exposed. But God exposes them, and often what we considered our strength becomes our weakness. If you reflect on your life in prayer and write down on a pad of paper what you believe are your virtues, in truth those are your weaknesses. Those very virtues are your sources of trouble. The only way to deal with this is to look to God and stop thinking about yourself.

No person can know how weak and unrighteous they truly are until they have been exposed by the Holy Spirit, and again, nobody cares to be exposed. In the Old Testament, Elisha prophesied to Hazael about how cruel he would be as the next king of Israel. Hazael said, "Is thy servant a dog, that he should do this great thing?" (2 Kings 8:13). Then he went home, put a pillow over his master's face, and smothered him to death.

Remember Peter, the bold fisherman and disciple who said, "Let everybody else run from you, Lord, I'll not." Looking at Peter, the Lord replied, "Before the cock crows twice, you will deny me three times." And we all know he did just that. Nobody realizes how unstable they are. That's why it is dangerous to trust our good habits. That's why it's dangerous to trust our virtue.

How, then, do we learn self-distrust? This distrust is indeed the work of God's hands. God has to bring us to a place where we trust only Him regardless of the situation. The best way to find out you are no good is that God flashes inspiration in your soul and suddenly lets you know. We all lie and were born with an inclination toward sin, and we can believe that, accept it, and teach it boldly to others. In fact, those who most trust themselves may yet be the ones who are often quoting that all of their righteousness is but filthy rags.

But it takes the Holy Spirit to truly help you see it. It takes the Holy Spirit to tell you about your weakness and open your eyes. Job is an illustration of this. God worked on him until the scorching began to bite into the soul of Job. Eventually the time came when Job said, "O God, I've been talking and talking and talking, but now I shut up. I put my hand over my mouth. I am vile, O God." When he had finally learned that lesson, God responded, "All right, Job, now pray for the rest of them." So Job prayed for his friends, and God gave him back twice as much.

Father, I've been so full of myself and didn't know it.
I yield everything to You and trust You to lead me in
the way of total surrender. Amen.

TRUST AND OBEY

When we walk with the Lord
in the light of his word,
what a glory he sheds on our way!
While we do his good will,
he abides with us still,
and with all who will trust and obey.

Trust and obey, for there's no other way
to be happy in Jesus, but to trust and obey.

Not a burden we bear,
not a sorrow we share,
but our toil he doth richly repay;
not a grief or a loss,
not a frown or a cross,
but is blest if we trust and obey.

Trust and obey, for there's no other way
to be happy in Jesus, but to trust and obey.

But we never can prove
the delights of his love
until all on the altar we lay;
for the favor he shows,
for the joy he bestows,
are for them who will trust and obey.

Trust and obey, for there's no other way
to be happy in Jesus, but to trust and obey.

Then in fellowship sweet
we will sit at his feet,
or we'll walk by his side in the way;
what he says we will do,
where he sends we will go;
never fear, only trust and obey.

Trust and obey, for there's no other way
to be happy in Jesus, but to trust and obey.

John H. Sammis

16

TEMPTATIONS BOOST
CHRISTIAN MATURITY

My brethren, count it all joy when ye fall into divers temptations; Knowing this, that the trying of your faith worketh
patience.

James 1:2–3

Today's Christians do not quite understand that God sometimes gives us harsh scorching in promoting our Christian
maturity. Observe your family while your children are growing up. If you give them nothing but sugar cookies to eat,
their teeth will be full of cavities by the time they reach twelve
years old. They must be given some healthy food.

To define these scorchings, I need to use the words *violent* and *insuperable* (impossible to overcome) regarding
such temptations. Most of us would rather hear words that
soothe, comfort, and make us feel good about ourselves. Yet

that could prove to be the formula for catastrophe in our Christian maturity.

When we are violently tempted and, for a moment, insuperably tempted, we are inclined to throw in the towel and say, "God, it's no use. I'm no good. I've read about D. L. Moody and St. Augustine and the rest, but I'm not like them. I'm no use to you, God; you don't want me. I'm finished." We forget that God wants to teach us about self-distress, sometimes through violent, insuperable temptations. When a temptation blows up on you that you thought was dead and buried years ago, instead of taking it as proof that you're not a Christian at all, you need to take it as proof that you're nearer to home today than you were yesterday, and that your heavenly Father is letting this thing happen to you to show you your weakness.

Brother Lawrence once said he always walked with the Lord. "If ever I make a slip anywhere, I never let it give me much trouble; I go straight to the Lord and say, 'Now, Lord, that's me. If you don't help me, that's what you can expect, for that's me.'" Brother Lawrence then thanked God for forgiving him and went right on from there.

Sometimes we are told by those trying to help us that repentance is a drawn-out affair wherein we must beat ourselves up for a long time. But there comes a time when we must realize that the best way to move forward is to turn toward God and not do the offending thing anymore. That's the best repentance in the world. If you did something yesterday you were ashamed of and are suffering under conviction and condemnation, you might ask, "How should I repent?" Turn to the Lord, confess your sin to Him, and then don't do it anymore.

Are temptations and failures proof that you are not a true Christian? No. They prove that your conscience is tender. You are very near to God, and the Lord is trying to teach you that last lesson of self-distrust by way of a violent temptation. Look at history. Remember Jacob's temptation? Remember Peter's temptation? We see that those temptations resulted in repentance and getting back in line with God.

Our heavenly Father wants to teach self-distrust by means not always understood by us. We pretend to know exactly what is going on when in fact we've no idea. We have a certain confidence in ourselves that is misplaced. A wise old saint once said, "Sometimes God teaches you self-distrust by His own mysterious methods, and you don't know what's happening to you."

God knows we do not know much, and so He lets things happen to us that we don't understand. You might go to somebody you trust who you feel is a saint, thinking that person will be able to tell you what's happening. You unload your heart to them, but they can't tell you anything. That is good, for it would be terrible if we had some holy St. Francis who everybody could go to and find out what was happening to them. God would not allow that. He loves you like no other, and He's trying to teach you to trust Him completely and not cling to people.

You may not understand the means God uses, but you are a Christian. Understand that, and love God. You are sick of all the nonsense in the world, and you are sick of all the nonsense in the Church. You're crying after God as the roe deer after the water brooks, and your heart longs for Him, the living God. Yet here is the obstacle: You still trust yourself. You are born again; you can testify to the truth of this. You love studying your Bible, you have a solid prayer life and are a good Christian, but you still trust yourself.

Others pat you on the back and say, "Glory to God, brother, you are born again," as if you already finished your journey. But the Lord says that's only the beginning. After we are born again, we are on the straight path to heaven, but we are also at the mercy of God's judgment in this life. God only judges when there is nothing else He can do to set us right. A lifetime of rebellion, unbelief, sin-loving, vileness, and refusal to obey are what bring judgment. When judgment falls, the Scripture says it's God's strange work. And He does not like to do it.

On the other hand, when God sends or allows violent and insuperable temptations, by harsh and strange means, you can rest assured that He is not judging you—He is watching you grow. If I could use such a word about God, I would say He is proud to see you grow. Zephaniah says, "The LORD thy God in the midst of thee is mighty; he will save, he will rejoice over thee with joy; he will rest in his love, he will joy over thee with singing" (Zephaniah 3:17).

If that is not a picture of a father singing over his family, I do not know what is. Deuteronomy 33:12 says, "The beloved of the LORD shall dwell in safety by him; and the LORD shall cover him all the day long, and he shall dwell between his shoulders." God picks us up and carries us, makes our bed in our sickness, understands our thoughts, and knows we are dust; and He is loving and patient toward us. God isn't angry. Because He wants His children to grow, sometimes He must chasten them. "For whom the Lord loveth he chasteneth, and scourgeth every son whom he receiveth" (Hebrews 12:6).

What, then, are we to do? We are to trust, love, and count on Him.

Do you know anybody you can count on completely? Do you know anybody you can count on even when you are in the wrong? We can all count on our friends if we are right. But suppose we are wrong. Do you know anyone you can count on then? A prominent French preacher once said, "My friends would fill this great cathedral, but my real friends would occupy these few seats here." He was not a cynic; he was being honest.

Who can you count on when you are not right? I can tell you, and His name is Jesus. You have to trust the Lord completely and let Him do His work in you. Do not push back, do not struggle, do not say, "God, you gotta do it now." If you are in the hands of God and obeying Him, He will lead you. And He will never, ever let you down. Keep looking to Jesus, behold Him high and lifted up, and remember that He is there triumphant.

The only way we will get to that place where we trust Him implicitly with everything about our life is through our trials and temptations. James understood this when he wrote in his epistle, "My brethren, count it all joy when ye fall into divers temptations; knowing this, that the trying of your faith worketh patience. But let patience have her perfect work, that ye may be perfect and entire, wanting nothing" (James 1:2–4).

Many Christians today believe joy comes when everything goes their way, when life is exactly how they want it. That was not the way James saw it, and this is not how we are to see it if we're going to grow spiritually. James tells us to "count it all joy." It is hard to comprehend this because the following phrase says "when ye fall into divers temptations." James is encouraging the believers to be aware of the temptations that come our way, and when they do come, we are to embrace them with joy.

As a new Christian, I would get angry and lose my temper whenever temptations came my way. But as I grew spiritually, through the years I have learned that God allows temptations to come into my life for a purpose. I can focus on the temptation and try to beat it down as best I can, or I can look to see God's face shining in my direction. Temptation is one of the ways in which God accomplishes something in my life that only He can do.

James points out that when temptation comes our way, it is simply "the trying of your faith that worketh patience." He goes on to say, "But let patience have her perfect work, that ye may be perfect and entire, wanting nothing." In other words, let the temptation run its course because God is doing something in your life that you probably do not understand. When that temptation has done the work that God assigned it, James tells us, "Ye may be perfect and entire, wanting nothing." What a beautiful purpose it serves.

As we grow in the grace and knowledge of Christ, temptations take on different levels. When I was a Christian initially, those temptations seemed very difficult at the time, but compared to today, they were not that hard. Still, the temptations back then were doing in my life what God assigned them to do.

When one temptation had completed its work, another was soon on its way to me. Personally, it took me a long time to get into "rejoice mode" whenever temptations came my way. Even today, I find it difficult to rejoice over temptation, but I trust that God is helping me to grow in Him.

Heavenly Father, amid my temptations I enthusiastically rejoice in Your Son, Jesus Christ. My temptations are but a door that can bring me closer to Thee in my Christian maturity. Amen.

YIELD NOT TO TEMPTATION

Yield not to temptation,
For yielding is sin;
Each vict'ry will help you,
Some other to win;
Fight valiantly onward,
Evil passions subdue;
Look ever to Jesus,
He will carry you through.

Ask the Savior to help you,
Comfort, strengthen and keep you;
He is willing to aid you,
He will carry you through.

Shun evil companions,
Bad language disdain;
God's name hold in rev'rence,
Nor take it in vain;
Be thoughtful and earnest,
Kindhearted and true;
Look ever to Jesus,
He will carry you through.

Ask the Savior to help you,
Comfort, strengthen and keep you;
He is willing to aid you,
He will carry you through.

To him that o'ercometh,
God giveth a crown;
Through faith we will conquer,
Though often cast down;
He who is our Savior,
Our strength will renew;
Look ever to Jesus,
He will carry you through.

Ask the Savior to help you,
Comfort, strengthen and keep you;
He is willing to aid you,
He will carry you through.

H. R. Palmer

17

THE ENVIRONMENT OF CHRISTIAN MATURITY

But seek ye first the kingdom of God, and his righteousness; and all these things shall be added unto you.

Matthew 6:33

God created man in His image, and no other creature is thus spoken of. I cannot find anywhere in the Scriptures God saying He created the seraphim in His image, nor the cherubim with all their faces and wings—nor any angel, archangel, principality, or power. Rather, God said affectionately, "Let us make man in our image" (Genesis 1:26). So in His image God created man and blew into him the breath of life, and man became a living soul.

As originally created, then, man was more like God because no other creature did God say He made in His image. The German theologian Meister Eckhart said, "There is nothing in the universe so much like God as the human soul." Of course, man's soul became sinful and lost, and in that sense, sin is not like God and the soul that sins shall die. And yet there remains something fundamental in human nature and the soul of man that can become more like God than anything else in the universe. I only wish we could accept that and not be afraid that if we say we believe it, somebody will charge us with believing that man is all right. Man is not all right. Man is a fallen creature; man is lost.

But God created man to know Him, and to know Him in a sense and to a degree that no other creature can. The other creatures in God's presence cannot know God as well as the soul of a man, which God has made in His image. There has to be a degree of life there that enables a man to know God.

Consider your cat or dog, resting quietly at home. Put on a record by Mozart or Beethoven, and they will never open their eyes because nothing in their nature can relate to Beethoven or Mozart. Put on the records of the best choirs singing Christmas carols. No cat or dog will pay them any mind. They can't appreciate the music, because they do not have the kind of life to appreciate it.

With our two-year-old baby, we thought he was unusual because when we played music, he would sway his little body. Then we found out all babies do that. Every human being is like this; it is built into them by God, who put music into the rhythm of His universe. He is the great musician. Babies are born into this stream like fish are born in the water. As they grow and become aware of music, they smile and sway to it because it is the dance of life. And it is God who gave them that kind of nature.

God made us to know Him in a way no other creature can know Him because no other creature shares the same capacities as man. Certainly the angels have capacities. There are holy angels who obey God. The seraphim around the throne shine in the fire of God, and they know God, but they don't know God as a man can know Him when redemption has been completed. God means that man should be higher than the angels. Yet God made man a little lower than the angels (Hebrews 2:7) so that He might raise him higher than the angels. Therefore, when it is all over and we know as we are known, we shall rank higher in the hierarchy of God than the very angels themselves. This is the foundation of our life here on earth.

It was because of Adam and Eve's disobedience in the Garden of Eden that man fell into depravity and lost that connection with God. By his sin, man lost this knowledge. The apostle Paul wrote, "Because that, when they knew God, they glorified him not as God, neither were thankful; but became vain in their imaginations, and their foolish heart was darkened" (Romans 1:21). This means they did disgraceful acts, so that man by his sin lost the knowledge of God. So now, man, though he has the potential to know God in a way no other creature in heaven and earth can, still does not know God because his conduct is unworthy of his high origin, and his heart is filled with a huge emptiness.

What is the matter with us? We have been told that science, philosophy, psychiatry, psychology, sociology, and so on should make the world a better place in which to live, that we could all be brothers. But we hate each other more than ever. There is as much hatred, suspicion, betrayal, spying, espionage, treachery, and selling out as ever since the beginning of the world. What's the matter?

It is simply because man is filled with a vast emptiness. He was created to know God, but by his sin he chose the gutter and would not have God in His knowledge. Man is like a bird shut in a cage or a fish taken from the water. We instinctively crave the image and miss it, the eternal being, the life, the light, the friend. That's what is the matter with us.

What does the Bible teach about sinners knowing God? It teaches that God can be known and that He has not abandoned the human race as He abandoned the angels who sinned. Why did He abandon those angels? Because they were never made in the image of God in the first place. They were creatures capable of moral and spiritual perception, yet they were not made in the image of God. Because man was made in God's image, God gave man a chance by sending the Redeemer.

The Bible teaches that man can know God in Christ and through Christ, for He is the image of the invisible God, the brightness of His glory, and the expressed image of His person. The church fathers in the Nicene Creed said this about Him: "We believe in one Lord Jesus Christ, the only Son of God, begotten from the Father before all ages, God from God, Light from Light, true God from true God, begotten, not made; of the same essence as the Father. Through him all things were made." This is what the Bible teaches—that everything the Godhead is, Christ is.

Do not listen to those who say that God revealed himself through Christ, that Christ reflected more of God than others. Some water Christ down by claiming that certain individuals turn to God in a way that others do not. They say Jesus Christ was the supreme religious genius, catching and reflecting more of God than any other man. Don't listen to that because all it amounts to is insulting Jesus Christ.

Christ was not a reflector of deity only, though he was certainly that. He was not a revealer of deity only, though he was that too. He was, always has been, and never can cease to be God, the light of light, very God of very God, begotten, not created. All that the Godhead is, Christ is. So to know Jesus Christ is to be back at the ancient fountain again.

Go back to knowing God for yourself all over again, back to where Adam started and beyond where Adam started. Back beyond where the world began. Beyond where the angels began. Back to that ancient glory. In Jesus Christ, we leave all our current environments and return to the ancient source of our being.

In his hymn, Philip Doddridge wrote, "Now rest, my long-divided heart! / Fixed on this blissful center, rest; / Here have I found a nobler part, / Here heavenly pleasures fill my breast." Back at the ancient source of our being, we find the beginnings and start all over in Christ.

"That I may know him," said the apostle Paul. Why is it that Christians know Christ and God so little? Of course, man cannot know everything about the Godhead. Not all of the Godhead can ever be known because to know all of the Godhead, we would need to be on par with the Godhead. Just like you can't pour a quart of water into a pint vessel, you can't pour all of the Godhead into an experience of anyone who is less than God.

The ancient fathers, arguing for the Trinity, said, "God, the eternal Father, is an infinite God, and his name is love, and he is love." The very nature of love is to give itself away. He could not fully give His love to anyone who was not equal to Him. We have the ancient Son, who was equal to the Father. The eternal Father poured out His love into the Son, who could contain all of it because He is equal to the Father. Then these wise brethren reasoned that for the ancient Father to pour His love out on His Son would mean that a medium of communication had to be equal to the Father and the Son, and that was the Holy Spirit. There you have the Trinity. In the fullness of His love, the Father poured himself through the Holy Spirit, who is equal to Him, and to the Son, who is equal to the Spirit and the Father.

The limitless, infinite sea of being we call God—filling, surrounding, unfolding, and upholding—all that can be known of God is revealed in Christ. When Paul said, "That I may know him, that I may make him known," these words are not intellectual. We don't know God as we know the multiplication table or Morse code. Paul meant knowing Him by experience, consciously. He meant knowing God personally, Spirit touching spirit, heart touching heart.

This does not describe the carnal Christian, who knows God mostly by hearsay. Many in the Church tend to know God in this way only. Others may know Him, but only faintly. They have heard but faint echoes of God's voice instead of hearing the voice of God directly. You can always tell a man or a woman who has been in God's presence. There is a vibrancy in their testimony you won't find anywhere else.

I am concerned that many Christians do not personally know God. We have church attendance, fellowship, singing, and the continual support of one another. We lean on each other, engage in social interaction, religious activities, and use many different spiritual tools. And it's true that Jesus said that He needed to care for others, which included healing, raising from the dead, opening eyes, teaching, and bestowing blessings on them. However, He also had a solid and personal understanding of God as a person. When He went to the mountain to pray and wait on the Almighty God, He did not feel alone because God was there with Him.

Often in our modern Christian service, it's do this and do that, go here and go there. The result is that many of us know God only by hearsay. We want things instead of God. You see, God wants to give himself. God wants to impart himself with His gifts. Separated from God, every gift becomes dangerous. If I were to pray for all seventeen gifts mentioned in the epistles of Paul, the gifts of the Spirit, and I received them all, it would be dangerous to me so long as in the giving, God did not give himself with them. God wants to give us himself.

Isn't it true that when God creates an order of life, He creates an environment for that life? The oceans and lakes are the environment for whales and fish of all types. The air is the environment for the birds. The earth is the environment for the various animals. But the heart of God is the environment for the Christian. God meant that we should live in that environment. The great grief in heaven is that we want God's gifts but don't want God.

We must reject the modern trend of looking to God only for what we can get from Him. We are taught what we can get out of God and how we can get it, but the all-powerful God desires to be adored and admired for who He is. Yet that makes up only a portion of the overall picture. He also wants us to understand that with Him, we have everything else. Jesus said it another way: "But seek ye first the kingdom of God, and his righteousness; and all these things shall be added unto you" (Matthew 6:33).

I must confess, dear Lord, that my desires in the past have been detrimental to my spiritual growth and relationship with Thee. I repent and so desire Thee for Thyself and nothing more. Amen.

MY HEART IS FULL OF CHRIST

My heart is full of Christ, and longs
this glorious matter to declare!
Of him I make my loftier songs,
I cannot from his praise forbear;
my ready tongue makes haste to sing
the glories of my heavenly King.

Fairer than all the earth-born race,
perfect in comeliness thou art;
replenished are thy lips with grace,
and full of love thy tender heart:
God ever blest! we bow the knee,
and own all fullness dwells in thee.

Charles Wesley

18

An Important Door to Christian Maturity

If we confess our sins, he is faithful and just to forgive us our sins, and to cleanse us from all unrighteousness.

1 John 1:9

As Christians, we often do not give much thought to forgiveness. We have come to believe that if we have accepted Christ as our Savior, our sins are forgiven, and we no longer have to deal with that.

But John says something essential here about our Christian maturity. He starts with the troubling word *if*. Everything rests upon that word. God's faithfulness is already at work, and we can experience His full forgiveness—that is, "if we confess our sins." For God has done everything necessary for our divine forgiveness and pardon. There is nothing more

God needs to do to guarantee the forgiveness of our sins. Everything rests, then, on our willingness to confess them.

Sometimes we think that our sin, whatever it is, is really not that bad. "After all," you say, "I didn't rob a bank or murder anybody." Our trouble is that we do not comprehend what sin is to God. Rather, we group sin according to our categories so we can somehow manage it. But this is not the right way to look at sin, as you can see by reading the Scriptures, both Old and New Testaments. Growing in our Christian experience is largely facilitated by forgiveness, and even though we identify as Christian, we still sin. And since we sin, we require forgiveness.

I find that God is more willing to forgive us than we are to repent. I think of David and the terrible situation with Bathsheba. After all of that was over, Nathan the prophet went to David and confronted him about his spiritual condition. He pointed a finger at David and said, "Thou art the man" (2 Samuel 12:7).

I'm sure Nathan expected David to react in anger and attack him. Nevertheless, with boldness he revealed God's word to David. Nathan feared God more than he feared David. Because David was king, he had the power and authority to do whatever he wanted. We see, however, that when David was confronted with his sin, he immediately fell on his knees and sought the forgiveness of God. And God was willing to forgive David the moment David was willing to confess.

Why does God forgive sin? He forgives sin because it is a shadow between Him and us. If we are ever going to know God and grow in Him, that shadow must be removed. Why does God pour out His Spirit on us when we trust Him and believe that He will do so? John 16:14 says, "He shall glorify me: for he shall receive of mine, and shall shew it unto you." But in order for God to show himself to us as fully as He wants to, the matter of our sin has to be dealt with.

When everything is clear between God and us, we are then in a position for God to reveal himself as we have never seen Him before. The most precious component in our Christian maturity is the smiling face of God looking at us, and sin robs us of that experience. Forgiveness brings us into harmony with God and His will. It brings us to a place where we can receive everything God wants us to receive.

Go back to Adam and Eve in the Garden of Eden. In the cool of the day, God would come and walk with them and fellowship with them. I do not know about you, but I would have loved to have been part of that fellowship. What did God say to them, and what did they have to say to God? Remember, Adam and Eve were perfect at that point, and sin had not yet invaded their relationship with God.

When God forgives you, He instantly wipes away anything and everything that has come between you and Him. To "let be backward," we need to continue to confess our sin to God. As we do this, allowing Him to forgive us of our transgressions, God promises through His grace to help us move forward in Him. It is rather strange that some people do not seem to want to be forgiven. They say they do, but in reality they hang on to their state of unforgiveness by ceasing to confess sin. Yet it is when we live and walk in His forgiveness that we come to know the Lord in new, rich, deep, and wonderful ways. This should be our passion: to seek God always. Then, when we find God, we seek Him all the more.

O God, I humbly confess my sins to You and ask for Your forgiveness. I gladly repent and embrace the forgiveness You have provided through Your Son, Jesus Christ. Amen.

LOVE DIVINE, ALL LOVES EXCELLING

Love divine, all loves excelling,
joy of heav'n to earth come down,
fix in us Thy humble dwelling;
all Thy faithful mercies crown!
Jesus, Thou art all compassion,
pure, unbounded love Thou art;
visit us with Thy salvation;
enter every trembling heart.

Breathe, O breathe Thy loving Spirit
into every troubled breast!
Let us all in Thee inherit,
let us find the promised rest.
Take away our love of sinning;
Alpha and Omega be;
end of faith, as its beginning,
set our hearts at liberty.

Come, Almighty to deliver;
let us all Thy life receive;
suddenly return and never,
nevermore Thy temples leave.
Thee we would be always blessing,
serve Thee as Thy hosts above;
pray, and praise Thee without ceasing,
glory in Thy perfect love.

Finish, then, Thy new creation;
pure and spotless let us be;
let us see Thy great salvation
perfectly restored in Thee.
Changed from glory into glory,
till in heav'n we take our place,
till we cast our crowns before Thee,
lost in wonder, love, and praise.

Charles Wesley

19

The Devil's Attack on Christian Maturity

For a just man falleth seven times, and riseth up again: but the wicked shall fall into mischief.

Proverbs 24:16

I sometimes sense a mysterious struggle, combat, wound, or pain, and I believe this is the conflict of Jesus being relived in His people. As they're moving into maturity, some experience a blessed, happy experience of God, while others feel the conflict as if a hot breath that is singeing them, and they know they have been where the devil is. I do not like the devil. I do not want to fight. I am not particularly eager to pray when I can smell brimstone. And I do not like to meet the devil in prayer, but I will if necessary. God help me not to run from it.

There exists in the world a dark and sinister enemy named the devil, Satan, or that old foe who is dedicated to the damnation of human souls. However, I think even the devil knows there's no use in trying to damn a Christian soul. The devil understands that when a child of God is secure in the hands of God, then justification and salvation are theirs. But even though the devil knows he cannot damn the Christian, he still wants to keep the Christian's spirit imprisoned. His main business with believers, then, is to keep their spirits in chains. If he can't prevent the Christian from being alive, he aims to have them so wound up in graveclothes that they might as well be dead. The devil's ultimate goal here is to rob them of the freedom they have in Christ.

I do not believe that Christians can be possessed by evil spirits. Yet they can be oppressed, intimidated, silenced, and repressed. Such is the devil's own handiwork.

Some Christians are childishly happy about everything it seems, for they have never been far enough along in their journey with God to know better. They are like children playing in the marketplaces. However, once the person gets serious about spiritual maturity and determines to have all that God has for them on earth, they are up against the devil. And he will not let them off easy.

We are frightened sheep without question, and yet we have every reason to be bold in Christ. Jesus came down and took our bodies on himself. He was a man born of a woman, a man wearing our nature. He was also God, and yet He embraced the cross. The Almighty God sacrificed His Son as the final fulfillment in summation of all the sacrifices made on Jewish altars.

After three days in the grave, Jesus rose from the dead and later ascended to the right hand of the Father, encompassed by the acclamations of the heavenly hosts. He sits at God's right hand, a living man, our representative there. We ought to be the most fearless, relaxed, happiest, most utterly God-assured people in the wide world, but instead many of us are not because we have allowed the devil to intimidate us.

Much like Goliath, who said, "I defy the armies of Israel," the devil's sinister, sour voice is saying cynically, "I defy you Christians." What can we do? Too often we behave like a flock of frightened sheep, but what exactly are we afraid of? And what are some of the things the devil uses to challenge our freedom as Christians? As mentioned, number one is our fear of our past sins. Sin is a terrible thing. God knows it, we know it, and the devil knows it, which is why he likes to follow us around—to remind us of our past sins.

Perhaps we need to talk back to the devil and say, "Yes, devil, sure I've sinned in the past, but I got it from you." Everything against us we got from the devil, while all that is good we get from Jesus Christ. This devil wants to keep us condemned, and if we get born again despite of him, he switches to trying to keep us shut in a little cage with our wings clipped so we can never fly. We claim our sins are gone, but many of us have a difficult time believing it. We sing, "Arise, my soul, arise, shake off thy guilty fears," yet we still walk around shackled by those memories.

When God forgives a man, He doesn't say to himself, "Now, let's watch this fellow because he has a bad record." Instead, He looks at that man and starts anew as if he had just been created and as if there were no past.

Another thing the devil uses to challenge our freedom is our memories of our failures. Satan would have you never forget them. After you fail, Satan will come and say, "You made a big to-do about the deeper life, about wanting to be filled with the Spirit and live the life in the Spirit. But look at all the flops you have made. Look how many times you've bruised yourself stumbling around."

The devil does not want you to remember God's Word, which says, "For a just man falleth seven times, and riseth up again: but the wicked shall fall into mischief" (Proverbs 24:16). I challenge you to research the saints of the past, starting with the biblical ones, and try to find just one who never made a terrible mistake. I looked at many of these and found that each one showed weaknesses and faults at some point in their life. But not enough for them to fail in such a way that would challenge God's ability and willingness to forgive them.

Did you not know that God, when He saved you, knew what kind of a person you were? Listen to the words of Isaiah: "Yea, thou heardest not; yea, thou knewest not; yea, from that time that thine ear was not opened: for I knew that thou wouldest deal very treacherously, and wast called a transgressor from the womb" (Isaiah 48:8).

The devil says, "Ah, but God doesn't know you like I do. He hasn't watched you as I have. Remember that time . . . ?" That's the devil talking. But God continues on and says, "I knew you that you would deal treacherously, and you were called a transgressor from the womb. But for my name's sake I will defer my anger, and for my praise will I refrain for thee. Behold, I have refined thee. I've chosen thee in the furnace of affliction. I will do it for my own sake" (9–11).

The devil does not want you to know that God has a stake in you. For his own sake, He will hold on to you. Don't you think God knew that you were treacherous? He knows the blood of Adam runs in your veins, and it is tainted blood. Again, God says, "I knew you were treacherous, but I was doing this thing for my own sake." Look away from yourself. God will bless you for Jesus' sake and for the sake of His glorious name. In fact, there is nothing that God will not do for you for His own sake.

Refrain, therefore, from letting your past failures get you down, even though they be many. You have made a fool of yourself, and your testimony has been punctured, flattened, and spoiled. Do not let that stop you. God knows everything about you. Ultimately, you are not responsible to men; you stand responsible before your heavenly Father and Jesus Christ at the right hand of God. Do not let your failures contaminate your freedom in Him.

The devil uses our weaknesses to compromise our freedom so that we never fully mature as Christians. As a result, our weakness goes unnoticed, and we don't recognize temptations when they come. If we don't resist temptation, our spiritual maturity is then compromised.

Nobody knew this as well as the apostle Paul when he said, "And he said unto me, My grace is sufficient for thee: for my strength is made perfect in weakness. Most gladly therefore will I rather glory in my infirmities, that the power of Christ may rest upon me. Therefore I take pleasure in infirmities, in reproaches, in necessities, in persecutions, in distresses for Christ's sake: for when I am weak, then am I strong" (2 Corinthians 12:9–10).

At the beginning of my ministry, my mother-in-law gave me some good advice I did not understand at the time. She said, "Be willing to be a fool for Jesus' sake." This sounded silly to a young man who did not want to be a fool, but wanted only to be a fine preacher. But as time went on, I came to appreciate the wisdom of her advice and have tried to live by it. Most Christians are not willing to be fools for Jesus' sake. The carnal Christian strives to appear respectable and smooth. Such "respectable Christians" will never get to where they should be spiritually until God delivers them from their notions of respectability.

Finally, always remember that the devil is a liar, the father of lies. He never tells the truth except when he can use it to intimidate and embarrass you. The only truth he tells is to remind us how much we have sinned and about our failures and weaknesses. The devil takes that truth and twists it, using it to try to destroy us. If we let go of our past, all our failures and mistakes, and accept God's mercy and forgiveness, that in itself will anger the devil.

As we grow in the grace and knowledge of the Lord Jesus, our freedom as Christians will be challenged every step of the way. But these challenges can lead us to a point of victory and greater freedom in Christ Jesus.

Heavenly Father, there are times when my past haunts me. I know that is the devil trying to separate me from You and Your forgiving love. I praise You that my past is completely forgiven and forgotten through the blood of Christ. Amen.

ARISE, MY SOUL, ARISE

Arise, my soul, arise,
shake off thy guilty fears.
The bleeding Sacrifice
in my behalf appears.
Before the throne my Surety stands;
before the throne my Surety stands,
my name is written on His hands.

He ever lives above,
for me to intercede;
His all-redeeming love,
His precious blood to plead,
His blood atoned for all our race,
His blood atoned for all our race,
and sprinkles now the throne of grace.

Five bleeding wounds He bears,
received on Calvary;
they pour effectual prayers,
they strongly plead for me.
"Forgive him, O forgive," they cry,
"Forgive him, O forgive," they cry,
"nor let that ransomed sinner die!"

My God is reconciled,
His pard'ning voice I hear;
He owns me for a child,
I can no longer fear.
With confidence I now draw nigh,
with confidence I now draw nigh,
and "Father, Abba, Father," cry.

Charles Wesley

20

LIVING IN THE FULLNESS OF CHRISTIAN MATURITY

Let us therefore, as many as be perfect, be thus minded: and if in any thing ye be otherwise minded, God shall reveal even this unto you.

Philippians 3:15

The journey to Jesus Christ is not made with our feet but with our hearts. Our feet can be anywhere, but only our hearts can make the journey to Him. In the New Testament, we have the story of Mary and Martha. The Scriptures tell us how Martha loved Jesus, but her concept of love centered on activity. Therefore, she was active, believing she should always be doing something if she loved the Lord Jesus. Mary, too, loved the Lord, but her understanding of the concept of love was quite different from Martha's. Mary was fervently occupied *in spirit* as she sought to love Jesus.

Many Christians have a Martha syndrome, which is to say they are activity-based. They must always be doing something. It seems they are on the run continually; they feel if they are not attending an event or engaged in some activity or another, they are going nowhere in life. Like Martha, such people tend to believe that nonstop activity is both spiritual and good. Get them together and they will think up things to do, and then do them in the name of the Lord. Martha loved Jesus, but she thought the way to show it was never to sit down. Never stop. Just go, go, go all the time.

Those ones on the road toward Christian maturity have a Mary syndrome, which is focused on the person of the Lord Jesus Christ. Uppermost in Mary's mind and heart was that God should be loved, worshiped, and this was more important than anything else.

In coming to Jesus, we can be one of two kinds of Christians. We can be the external Christian who lives outside of oneself, not knowing much about their inner life, or we can be the internal Christian who lives from a wholly different place. When Jesus told the disciples to go into all the world and preach the gospel to every creature, Peter jumped up as if to get started at once. The Lord stopped him and said, "Not yet, Peter. Don't go like that. Tarry until you are imbued with power from on high, and then go."

Church leaders often tell new Christians to get busy sharing the gospel with others, but the Lord did not teach that. He wants them to learn to worship and praise Him and to have a transforming experience of the heart. Once this is established, then they are to go into the world to share the gospel message with the lost.

The most important thing for a person to do in this world—above all else, whether it be physical or spiritual—is to be fervently occupied with the love of Christ, to be focused on Him and develop a life of worship. Out of this will spring deep, enduring, and divine activity.

We must understand that virtue is nothing but an ordained and measured affection directed to God himself. What does it mean to be spiritual, to be maturing in your Christian experience? It is not a flash of spiritual feeling or emotion. You don't get goose bumps necessarily. It is more than that; it's an ordained and measured affection.

Do not try too hard to imitate others in your longing for God and in your desire to know Him. Everyone is imperfect. In *The Imitation of Christ*, Thomas à Kempis wrote, "If thou were to have peace of heart, inquire not earnestly into other men's matters." Do not examine your Christian brother or sister too closely if you want peace of heart because you will find things wrong with them. All idols, all people, have clay feet. Do not stumble over them.

God does not want us to become a worshiper of others. Instead, He wants to deliver us from people. He wants to deliver you from the best man or woman you know. Then, if that person should backslide, it will not change you in the slightest or distract you from pursuing your Christian maturity. Or if that person should die, there will not be any part of you that dies with them. You will remain the same, following the Lord faithfully. The devil delights in using the saints' imperfections to keep us from going forward in

Christ. Do not stumble over them as though that were the measure of one's spiritual maturity.

There is another stumble we need to keep in mind, and that concerns the praises of other people. The praises of others may well be more dangerous to the earnestly seeking Christian than their blame. Watch for this, because if the devil can get you to think you are in any way superior to your fellow Christians, he has got you hooked already. Also, as you seek God, resist judging the people you meet on your path to Him. The devil sees those you come in contact with and is sure to whisper to you, "That poor brother there, he's not the warmhearted Christian you are, is he?" And if you don't watch it, you will nod and say to yourself, "No, he isn't. I am a better Christian."

Continue to press forward, then, in your Christian maturity, being always vigilant about the praise and criticism of others as well as passing judgment on them. In *The Cloud of Unknowing*, the man of God said, "And therefore me thinketh, that they that set them to be contemplatives should not only have active men excused of their complaining words, but also me thinketh that they should be so occupied in spirit that they should take little heed or none what men did or said about them."

He encourages us to be so occupied in spirit that we ignore completely what people say about us. Is it not strange that nobody will bother you so long as you remain frozen in your seat and make no spiritual progress? But as soon as you start to cross the River Jordan, there will be fourteen people who begin to pray for you for fear you're losing your mind.

Every inch of ground we take away from the devil, we've got to take away with bleeding fingernails and sore knees.

Perhaps that is why we take so little ground from him. But if we're going to "look now forward and let be backward," it will cost us everything. To become a mature Christian in today's world is our greatest challenge.

I praise You, Holy Spirit, for urging me forward in Your direction. I am determined to yield each day to Your leadership and guidance. I long to experience that fullness that only You can bring to my heart. Amen.

THE FULNESS OF CHRIST

A fulness resides in Jesus our Head,
And ever abides to answer our need;
The Father's good pleasure has laid up in store
A plentiful treasure, to give to the poor.

Whate'er be our wants, we need not to fear;
Our numerous complaints his mercy will hear;
His fulness shall yield us abundant supplies;
His power shall shield us when dangers arise.

The fountain o'erflows, our woes to redress,
Still more he bestows, and grace upon grace.
His gifts in abundance we daily receive;
He has a redundance for all that believe.

Whatever distress awaits us below,
Such plentiful grace will Jesus bestow
As still shall support us and silence our fear,
For nothing can hurt us while Jesus is near.

When troubles attend, or danger, or strife,
His love will defend and guard us through life;
And when we are fainting and ready to die,
Whatever is wanting, his grace will supply.

John Fawcett

21

THE TRIUMPH OF CHRISTIAN MATURITY

Jesus Christ the same yesterday, and to day, and for ever.

Hebrews 13:8

During my ministry in West Virginia, I picked up a piece of paper I found on a muddy road. I do not know who put it there, but I'm sure God sent me to see it. These words were scribbled on the paper: "There are only two things known to the universe that are bigger when they're born than when they get their growth. One is a wasp, and the other is a church member."

I don't know about the wasp, but I know many church members who started with a blaze and then looked around them to see that this was not the way to be a Christian, that it was not the way to act. They settled down and thanked the Lord for what they had in Jesus. Soon they are just as badly backslidden as the rest, only it is called by another name. You can die of cancer and call it by a beautiful Latin phrase that rolls off the tongue. Nevertheless, you are dead. Likewise, we can be backslidden and never know it.

My heart aches for carnal Christians, and I pray that something will compel them to wake up and find the path to pursuing Christian maturity. Conversely, I am enthusiastic about the mature Christians and their thirst for God. I pray that God will continue fueling that thirst every hour of every day. The carnal Christian is looking for what God can give them, while the mature Christian is seeking God for himself.

What we have going for us is that Jesus doesn't change: "Jesus Christ the same yesterday, and to day, and for ever." There is nothing Jesus ever did for any of His twelve disciples that He would not do for any of His other disciples, then and now. I find nothing in the Bible that says the Lord has changed anything. So, He never did anything for His disciples that He would not do for you. You will find Him just the same.

For instance, He is the same toward the proud. Prideful people did not get anywhere with Jesus when they came to Him. Jesus had all of God's mercy, grace, and love, but have you ever noticed that the proud never found that side of Him? Rather, they received judgment, justice, rebuke, and warning.

Today, too, you will find Jesus unchanged. Let a self-righteous man come to Him, and that man will receive the same rebuff he's always gotten. And if an insincere person comes to Him, they will get the same response. Our Lord Jesus Christ never listened to the insincere except to turn their words around and stick them with those words like a sword.

But I have happier news than this. He is the same Jesus toward the meek that He always was. He never turned away when a meek person came to Him. And His attitude toward those who mourn is the same as well. So is His attitude toward the repentant. The Lord never inquired how deep the sin was; He only inquired whether the sinner was sincere and repentant. If they were sorry for their sins and wanted to follow Him, to quit their sinful behavior, turn away from their sins and hate them, the Lord acted as if they had never committed any sin. Jesus is also the same toward the honest-hearted person, and He is the same toward those who love Him.

One aspect of God we do not hear much about these days is that the Lord Jesus Christ doesn't need us. God does not need us, nor does He need our talents. He is self-sufficient, which is one of His attributes. Though He does not need us, still He loves us and offers us His friendship.

With childlike faith, the apostle John rested his head against the beating heart of the Son of God, and the Lord loved that. They called John the disciple whom Jesus loved. Not that He didn't love the rest, but He couldn't love them as much because they didn't reciprocate as much as John did. You'll find Jesus just the same toward those who seek His company. People who seek Jesus' company want to be with Him always. And He wants those who are occupied with the love of His Godhead and who seek His company.

Jesus understands everything about you. He knew all about you before you were born. Therefore, if you come to Him self-confident and cocksure, you will find an icy reception.

But if you come to Him admitting you know nothing, you will find Him the sweetest teacher in the world. If you come to Him troubled, He stands ready to console the troubled heart. All we need is Jesus Christ. He will be your teacher while the world spins because He is infinite and God.

It was Paul who said, "Not as though I had already attained . . ." Paul, who had no righteousness of his own, pressed forward—in tears, pain, suffering, rebuff, persecution, tribulation, trouble, and woe. Still he said, "Not as though I had already attained, either were already perfect: but I follow after, if that I may apprehend that for which also I am apprehended of Christ Jesus" (Philippians 3:12).

Near the end of his time on earth, when Paul could finally say, "I fought the fight, I kept the faith, I've finished the race," the Lord let him bow his beloved neck. And the Roman sword whistled down and executed the man we now know as the apostle Paul. Yet did this bring an end to his life? No, for he had committed his life into the hands of Jesus. And when the sword came down, Paul never passed out of Jesus' hands.

I can only say with John the Baptist, "Behold the Lamb of God." Put your faith and trust in Him alone, then "look now forward and let be backward." Do not dwell on the past or allow yourself to stumble over your failures. Do not let anybody stop you as you seek the Lord and grow in Him. Like Paul, press forward in pursuing your Christian maturity.

Finally, look to Jesus for clearer light, He who is the same Jesus who gave the blind their sight and healed them. All we need is more of Jesus, and we can have more of Him. Let us remember His promise to His followers, then and now, today: "Be not afraid . . . I am with you always, even unto the end of the world" (Matthew 28:10, 20).

I claim my victory in Thee, O God. Only You can bring to me what You desire in me. I have fully surrendered to You. I don't know my future, but I know I can trust You to lead me down the right path for Your Name's sake. Amen.

FURTHER READING

A.W. Tozer drew from many sources on this topic. While we don't know exactly which editions he quoted, we've compiled a list of books he drew from if you'd like to do further reading:

The Cloud of Unknowing by Anonymous, late fourteenth century

The Inner Life by François Fénelon, 1853

On Watchfulness and the Guarding of the Heart by Nicephorus (Nikephoros), thirteenth century

Revelations of Divine Love by Dame Julian of Norwich, 1670

The Spiritual Combat by Lorenzo Scupoli, 1589

The Imitation of Christ by Thomas à Kempis, c. 1418–1427

A.W. Tozer (1897–1963) was a self-taught theologian, pastor, and writer whose powerful words continue to grip the intellect and stir the soul of today's believer. He authored more than forty books. *The Pursuit of God* and *The Knowledge of the Holy* are considered modern devotional classics. Get Tozer information and quotes at X.com/TozerAW.

Reverend James L. Snyder is a prolific, award-winning author and an authority on the life and ministry of A.W. Tozer. Because of his thorough knowledge of Tozer, James was given the rights from the A.W. Tozer estate to produce new books derived from over four hundred never-before-published audiotapes. He and his wife live in Ocala, Florida. Learn more at AWTozerClassics.com, and connect with James at JamesSnyder51@gmail.com or at JamesSnyderMinistries .com.